The Art of Economic Sanctions

Mohammadreza Ahang

2014/Oct

The Art Of Economic Sanctions

Mohammadreza Ahang © 2014

The Art Of Economic Sanctions

Title: The Art of Economic Sanctions

Author: Mohammadreza Ahang

Translator (from Persian):Mohammadreza Ahang

ISBN: 9781939123343

Publisher: Supreme Century, USA

Prepare for Publishing: Asan Nashr

To My Hero

- My Mother

Contents

Reference

Preface

Nowadays, The issue of Economic Sanctions to be changed for one of the most important Political-Economic challenges in the world, also some politicians Utilize the most complicated tools for achieving others accompaniment in order to advocate the interests of their countries.

Sanctions have long history (It returns to the Empire of Rome & Greece) and nowadays the countries like USA as well as European Union, For the sake of various reasons, prefer to use sanctions instead of war to change other countries' attitude (countries like Iran, Russia, Cuba, North Korea and ...). It is clear that Economic Sanctions are not the best solution in all cases, The history has shown that in some countries like Afghanistan, Iraq, ...the main purpose was war therefore sanctions in some cases are not the aim.

Regardless of whether Economic Sanctions is considered as a warm gun which hurt innocent societies

(Economic Sanctions is a kind of hidden war), This book has conducted survey the trend of Sanctions and related Economic Tools impartially. This book shows different aspects of Sanctions without any emotional interference which can be helpful to represent the points of strength and weakness. The academic level of subjects is considered for individuals with the average knowledge of Macroeconomics and The Game Theories.

This book in order to opt the best strategy by Sender (a country that impose Sanctions) and Target (a country that endure Sanctions), has Utilized The Game Theories and Economic parameters in Macroeconomics which can play pivotal function in our arguments. Also Sender & Target are general meaning and each country can be a Target or Sender, however, somewhere that examples can be helpful, it is necessary to review history and real examples.

This book is engaged in the Economic aspects of Sanctions whilst, obviously, the usage of other social science for saving coherence is unavoidable. Many books and articles have been studied to write this book which paved the way, with a view to the fact that all the results of this book by considering Macroeconomics is the consequence of author's notion, I would accept all responsibility about any scientific mistakes .

Mohammadreza Ahang

2014/oct.

Introduction

This book is engaged in the survey of various aspects of Economic Sanctions. Generally has two parts, in the first part has used the main parameters for acquiring positive results in the sanctions, in the second part has focused on Economic consequences of Sanctions.

Initially, we encounter with short summary of Sanction history which is important for beginning the argument. The aim of this chapter is understanding of why countries use Sanctions, also some results of Economic Sanctions can help to consolidate tie between theories and real world.

Then, with the assumption that a country shows insubordinate behavior, the main goals of Sanctions will survey. Each country has specific condition therefore the usage of a certain prescription for all is unwarranted. The main parameters in each countries can help making decision, also scale and scope of sanctions can choose by these factors.

Simulating and forecasting actions & reactions in Sanctions are so important because needed provision in Sanctions should be taken into consideration before any activity, hence, the best tool for this aim is The Game Theories.

The survey of Economic sides of Sanctions can reveal its costs and benefits which play main role in making decision and policy. Some parts of the book have used Macroeconomics to cover this issue.

Finally, Sanctions will consider as a Chess Game that players would follow the maximum of profits, thus some effective policies would help our argument.

Why & How to Use Economic Sanctions

1.History

Introduction

The history of Sanctions has Widespread aspects but at this historical review our aim is to become familiar with the area of Sanctions, Therefore it is clear that the book cannot encompass all countries which have endured Sanctions.

432 BC

For the first time Athens Impose Trade Sanctions on its neighbor (Megara) because of three women, kidnapping by citizens of Megara. Traders of Megara did not have permission to have activity in Athens' markets and harbor that this condition led to a war which annihilated new founded Democracy of Athens

1892-1894 AD

Through a series of conferences in Europe about ways that can oblige countries to obey international laws, Professor Henri La Fontaine had pivotal function to present subjects about Sanctions.

1918 AD

After The First World War, The politician of France, Léon Bourgeois, expressed his request based upon formation of the Society of nations by order to seclude countries which violate international laws.

1919 AD

The president of United States, Woodrow Wilson, supported a legal draft which used Sanction against citizens of hostile countries, in addition a ban on trade and disconnection with other members was solicited.

1935-1936 AD

The theory of Wilson defeated at the first great examination and was not able to persuade Italian army to retreat from Abyssinia. Italy was looking for a colony in Africa like other great authorities, hence Abyssinia was selected due to Economic goals and the consolidation of Government position. Initially, France as well as England tried to support Italy by virtue of the threat of Germany but for the sake of their colonies in Africa, decided to support the request of Abyssinia in Society of nations. A series of Sanctions against Italy was used which encompassed trade Sanctions and blocking the purchase of arms. However these sanctions were not comprehensive and all countries did not join this rally .

1940-1941 AD

USA imposed a ban on trade with Japan, thus this action motivated Japan to join The Second World War. In 1937, Japan attacked China because of the spread of authority in the south west of Asia, after awhile many victories acquired which had threaten USA and the west interests. Hence USA imposed a series of hard Sanctions and Japan after considerable negotiations was not able to dissuade USA and this reason was enough to persuade Japan to attack US army in Pearl Harbor .

1967 AD

Norwegian sociologist   John Galtung, criticized the prevailing view about comprehensive Economic Sanctions due to the probability of increasing people nationalism which can make leaders popular and this condition can hurt innocents.

1980 AD

In south Africa, The effect of international Sanctions against Apartheid was intensified by groups, protecting civil laws. About 20 billions $ was discharged from firms by people and staffs, thus Government encountered with an increasing pressure. Generally, the belief is that Sanctions were helpful for annihilating Apartheid, although the sheer volume of costs that Apartheid suffered, was from people and unsuitable domestic policy.

1990 AD

The Security Council after an invasion of Kuwait by Iraq, imposed the comprehensive Sanctions that for Sanctions against Haiti And Yugoslavia was inspiration. The president of Iraq after the war between Iran and Iraq, was confused by the sheer volume of debt which was taken from Arabic countries, In addition infrastructures of Iraq was damaged, therefore requested from Kuwait to donate its loan (about 30 billions $) thanks to the benefit of war which all Arabic countries had gained. Kuwait did not accept the request and with reciprocal action had tried to keep the price of oil at the low level which was unbearable for Iraq. These factors led to new war between Iraq and Kuwait which 20% of oil sources was at disposal of Iraq. Security council blocked assets of Iraq and then imposed Oil Sanction. These sanctions were introduction for new war (Persian Gulf War) that powerful countries like US defeated Iraq in Kuwait.

1993-1994 AD

The Security Council imposed severe Economic Sanctions against military groups who controlled government in Haiti. After military coup in 1991 and the dismissal of president Bertrand Aristide, American Countries Organization endeavored to achieve stability in Haiti but rebels thwarted their plan, therefore The Security Council imposed Sanctions on military sector, travelling and transportation. The Sanctions were inefficient, in addition several reviews of Sanctions along by intensification of international pressure were not deterrent. In 1994 an international military group ceased chaotic situation.

1995 AD

According to various evidences from the lateral damages of Iraq sanctions, unfortunately over a half million children were killed so that British ambassador David Hannay, warned UN that the assertion of smart sanctions cannot distinguish innocent. After awhile Iraq received food in return for oil.

1997-1999 AD

A model for impose smart sanctions on the rebels of Angola was designed by UN which imposed a ban on travelling and blocked the assets of rebels. In 1992, free elections was held in Angola which was confirmed by UN. According to the elections, Jose Eduardo Dos Santos was legal president but Jonas Savimbi did not accept the results of elections therefore this condition led to civil war in Angola.

2001 AD

After 11/September the president of US, George W.Bush used the comprehensive sanctions against terrorists and imposed a ban on all assets of this group.

2003 AD

Sweeping Sanctions against Baghdad was revoked just after two months from an invasion of Iraq by US but obviously, the Sanctions did not succeed to compel a change in behavior of Iraq about WMD.

2003-2004 AD

Sanctions against Libya in 1980's & 1990's was revoked because the leader of Libya Muammar Gaddafi, renounced terrorism and dismantled his WMD. This Sanction was among a few cases which was successful and coerced Target into changing its behavior.

2006 AD

After nuclear experiments by North Korea, Security Council imposed a series of Sanctions on North Korea that its aim was assets and luxury items, interested by the leader of North Korea Kim Jong IL.

2006-2009 AD

The head of treasury of US Stuart Levey, at a meeting with about 12 foreign banks, propounded his solicitation about Sanction against Iran.

2011-2012 AD

Countries like China reduced the effects of Oil Sanction and blocking the Central bank of Iran, on the other hand after passing a year from Smart Sanctions against Syria, president Bashar Asad said Syria does not depend on Oil income therefore Oil Sanction cannot affect Syria.

2. Stages of Using Economic Sanctions

Introduction

Sender(s) are looking for the optimization of condition through war or Sanctions. What would change the function of Sender(s) is total situation of their country and Target's country. Therefore at this chapter we will survey the stages of imposing Sanctions and factors which affect the trend of Sanctions. This trend encompass about 9 stages that Sender(s) would consider in their policy after each violation of standard behavior.

2.1 Goals of Sanction

However Economic Sanctions have been frequent throughout history but out of each 10 cases, only 3 cases have had reasonable results, hence it shows a kind of incongruent link between Sanctions and spots of weakness. The dilemma is always the same: why great authorities after unsuccessful experiences, use Sanctions continuously ?

Sanction is primary measure to compel a change in behavior of Target, or sets the stage for next action which can be military action. For instance, The Sanctions of Iraq were unsuccessful and behavior of Saddam Hosein did not change but the main goal was different, the Sanctions prepare convenient situation for war.

In 1967, Galtung said : Sanction is a kind of action which a country/countries use various tools in order to deprive Target of values and to coerce it into changing their behavior. Galtung reckoned that the probability of positive effectiveness of Economic Sanction is not considerable. In 1972 and 1985, Doxey and Baldwin respectively represented similar results by issuing some scientific essays. Nowadays results of Sanctions are noticeable that the share of success is low. The main purpose of Sanction is changing Target's behavior but it is of great importance to consider the role of Target from the viewpoint of political and economic functions in the world, because Sanction can change world order and the role of Target, thus changing economic and political ties can advocate the interests of Sender(s) thanks to a decrease in supply of goods and services (an increase in price), in addition Sender(s) can undertake an important role at the absence of Target's actions. On the other hand, in essence Sanction can improve status of Sender(s) among other countries by virtue of hegemony which can emerge from Sanctions.

Politicians in contrast with Economists believe that Economic Sanctions can act as powerful tools for achieving goals, obviously goals of Sanctions in terms of policy can hurt Economic goals in short-run. Diverse expected goals in Sanction will survey in the next part.

2.1.1 Obvious Goals

-Changing behavior : In some cases, Target's behavior can hurt the interests of other countries also lateral results of Target's activities can affect other countries in future. Therefore Sender(s) use Sanctions to cease Target's activities.

-Punishment against wrong policy : The policy of Target does not always have negative result, though there is a potential danger because of similar policies. Thus Deterrent Punishment can prevent a new challenge.

-Punishment because of breaking Sanctions : Sanctions cannot be successful if other countries do not collaborate with Sender(s) or at least it does not have starting effect on Target. Hence, punishment is a response to countries which have reciprocal relationship with Target.

-Reducing the pace of Target to achieve goals : Sanction has different levels and does not always use at the highest level because Targets have different effects on the world and the highest level of Sanction can hurt unaligned countries by decreasing the level of trade. Smart Sanctions can solve the problem with the minimum of lateral damage to other countries.

-Authorities instability : Countries with congruent policy can achieve optimum point after actions and reactions because each side can understand the profit of other side, but sometimes logic can be superseded by Ideology and negotiations lose their efficiently. Sender(s) would not able to consider a condition which achieve common grand with Target, therefore a putsch can change equations and Sanctions can help these kind of activities.

-**Destroying of military power** : According to some evidences which show an anomalous activity for Target's Army, Sender(s) sometimes decide to use a series of Smart Sanctions against military power.

-Protection of NGOs and Human right : Smart sanctions can coerce Governments into change their behavior against innocents people. Unfortunately some countries are wracked by a totalitarian political system that other countries can play an important role to protect people.

-**Prevention of forming multi-Governments in a country** : Instability and the absence of central Government in a series of countries lead to military rebel's activities, causing disasters. Thus Smart Sanctions can be helpful to defeat these groups.

2.1.2 Hidden Goals

-**Increasing of political power in district and the world** : Economic Sanctions against other countries, demonstrate political and economic dominance also lead to hidden fear of hegemony. This show can surge obedience to Sender(s) and it can pave the way for acquiring new interests in the world.

-Dominance of strategic goods' valve : A series of goods in the world like Oil, can challenge Economies. Therefore the control of supply of this strategic goods can confer considerable power on Sender(s) that the world price would determine by Sender(s) and a sheer volume of profit can be achieved.

-Preparation of war : Sanction is a tool which can utilize instead of war but in some cases it can play complementary role because Sanctions can damage the stability of Economy, policy and Army, hence such this suitable condition can help Sender(s) to defeat Target. On the other hand, breaking Sanctions can set the stage for new war because it shows rational reason for imposing a war.

2.2 *Effective Parameters in Sanctions*

Authorities' structure encompass Economy, Policy, Society, and Army is One of the most important factors that result in changing the kind of Economic Sanctions. Therefore it is of great necessity to study the effectiveness of parameters on Sanctions before any practical action because the probability of win in a cold war depends on suitable strategy, in addition each strong strategy can be achieved by enough awareness of the effective parameters.

The behavior of each country depends on various variables but here we try to use simple examples owing to understanding the connection between theory and real world. Clearly, The constancy of other condition is a necessary assumption.

2.2.1 Political & Military Structure

a) Military Power

Nowadays like other historical periods, the military power of each country can increase country's status therefore many international decisions depend on this capacity. Thus , the cooperation of countries in war and Sanctions depends on the military power of leader.

- **Sender(s)** : Throughout the history it can be seen that the military power was a main element for using Sanctions therefore Sender's army should be more powerful than Target's army to cripple adversaries.

- **Target :** After awhile that Target resist the pressure of Sanctions, Sender(s) would design a plan for martial condition because the cost of Sanction affects two sides of Sanction, thus Sender(s) want to achieve goals as soon as possible by military actions. Obviously, Target with powerful Army can increase the cost of Sender(s)' military action therefore the military power of Target can act as a deterrent.

-**Example :** The Army of North Korea against US has a deterrent power, so that long-run Sanctions and considerable expenditure cannot persuade US to attack this country (There are various factors lead to new condition of North Korea)

b) The school of policy

There are three different groups encompass : liberalism, socialism and religious ideology that each group has different reaction to Sanctions.

-Sender(s) : Liberal Countries which have election are under pressure of the public voice, therefore Government prefer Sanctions to war because it has undesirable effect on society. On the other hand socialist parties in compare with liberal parties, consider lower weight for the public voice. Thus the process of making decision is different that calculate obvious cost-benefit of war and Sanctions. Countries with religious ideology follow certain belief that make it foreseeable, in addition the cost and benefit has lower importance because the goals of these countries are generally different. Totally, religious countries try to make ideological front against their enemies.

-Target : Liberalism because of reciprocal affiliation with people, in long-run cannot tolerate the pressure of Sanctions. It is clear that economic pressure can increase protests so that Governments should be responsible. On the other hand socialism by regarding to its nature (The obedience of people) and relatively low level of life, has more power of resistance. The resistance of religious ideology depends on the amount of trust between people and authority. People of these countries believe celestial factors which can increase the patience of people in hard situations.

-Example : Iran as an ideological country has been suffered from Sanctions for the sake of his WMD, since 10 years ago. Today more than ever, authority want to solve the problem by negotiation with Senders because after these years people have been fractionally lost their belief about continuing this attitude.

c) Foreign policy

Sanctions would be effective if international players protect Sender(s), therefore foreign policy can provide an incentive for persuading other countries to joint rally so that The comprehensive Sanctions can acquire reasonable result.

-Sender(s) : The public voice throughout the world can affect the efficiency of Sanctions negatively and increase the political cost. Hence, the consolidation of political ties can prevent protestations in other countries.

-Target : an increase in political cost would affect Sender(s) and breaking Sanctions, therefore sufficient rapport between Target and unaligned countries can help to condemn Sanctions.

-Example : Iran has shown new foreign policy from 2013 to decline the challenges over the world which has led to an decrease in the volume of Sanctions.

d) Domestic policy

Economic Sanctions increase the cost of living in order to cripple Government. people would bear pressure of Sanctions in both sides, therefore authorities should choose a new domestic policy for keeping the peace of their countries.

-Sender : After each Sanctions, the potential of Economic opportunity in Target's country would be lost, on the other hand travelling between countries would be decreased. Therefore it is necessary that Government convince people to curtail their relation with Target.

-Target : Economic Sanctions lead to hard condition for living in Target, thus authorities try to give points as an incentive to people instead of a decrease in people's real revenue. It is clear that Government cannot entice people with economic motivation, therefore responsibility to political requisition can absorb support from people.

-Example : Cuba in 2010, released many political prisoners which resulted in compliments from US and opponents.

e) Political power in various district

The comprehensive Sanctions cut Economic relationship between a country and other countries. This condition would be occurred if all connections with other countries decline to the lowest level, such as water, ground and air. Therefore the political power of Target in neighbors can break Sanctions.

-**Sender(s)** : Neighbors of Target can play pivotal function for Sanctions because when neighbors joint Sender(s), goods and provisions would not pass border. Hence Economic pressure would not be offset by an illicit activities, although concessions for persuading neighbors should be noticeable.

-**Target** : The political power as well as military power in neighbors' territory can decrease regional cooperation with Sanctions and decline the effects of Sanctions on Target. Obviously, these facilities increase the cost of governorship.

-**Example** : Israel have imposed Sanctions on Gaza until 2012 which after Egypt's election because of the suitable relationship between two governments' of Gaza and Egypt , the border opened for the authority of Gaza and the pressure of Sanctions decreased.

f) History & political experience

Human societies have learned from history and its experiences, in addition have inspired from defeats and victories in order to advance their goals. Therefore there are various historical evidences which can help authorities to tackle the problems of Sanctions.

-Sender(s) : The experience of defeat in a war or Sanctions can increase the pressure of opponents and other parties in a new experience because society cannot bear the same events and people would not support politicians who are blameworthy. Therefore a bad experience about war or Sanction can prevent new challenge.

-Target : Political experience like civil disobedience and protests can work as alert system which shows that an increase of Economic pressure in a condition such as Sanction, increase the probability of the great protests which can weaken Government against Sanctions.

-Example : Sudan had experienced severe protests until 2011 which increase the influence of Sanctions and led to changes in authority.

2.2.2 *Economic Structure*

a) The level of inflation and unemployment

Economic Sanctions have negative influences on common economic opportunity which can survey through inflation and unemployment in both sides.

-Sender(s) : Sanctions would be successful if other countries join rally, although the cost of persuading other countries is considerable and Sender(s) should acquire this amount of money by rising tax. On the other hand Economic opportunity in Target would be lost, hence in short-run an increase in unemployment is one of the result of Sanctions (The volume of unemployment after Sanctions depends on the level of economic ties between Target and Sender(s)). Sanctions can be superseded by war because it can increase employment in War factories as well as related firms (Making decision between war and Sanctions has a complicated process and the constancy of other conditions is a main assumption in our arguments).

-Target : Sanctions lead to a decline in Finance and employment, on the other hand an decrease in imports and an increase in the expenditure of production result in high inflation. Generally, one of the results of Sanctions in Target is Stagflation which increase unsatisfactory conditions.

-Example : North Korea because of severe Sanctions, has encountered with Stagflation condition, moreover one of the person in power for the sake of insufficiency was sentenced to capital punishment.

b) The Economic power in the world

Countries in international relationships in terms of Economic power, have various levels of effectiveness. In addition, it is clear that Sender(s) have more Economic power and applicability in compare with Target. Dependency and Economic power in the world can crush Sanctions and vice versa.

-Sender(s) : Economic power of Sender(s) should be able to tolerate the Sanction condition because the comprehensive Sanction needs a great consensus to increase the efficiency of Sanction, this aim would be achievable if Sender(s) provide incentives to absorb countries and save their profits in the absence of Target.

-Target : Generally, the countries which affect the Economy of the world, can break Sanctions because international relationships design in terms of national interests, therefore impose Sanctions on powerful country may result in an international disaster.

-Example : US imposed Sanction on Russia in 2013 because of an intervention in Ukraine. It is clear that the stage of Russia among Energy supplier can cease the protection of European union from sanction.

c) Wealth

Victory in big challenges like Sanctions and war need to have considerable stack of wealth, therefore this factor can play important role in the beginning of a sanction and over the period of resistance.

-**Sender(s)** : In short-run and at the beginning of Sanction in order to show positive signals to their alliance and persuade them to joint rally, sender(s) should spend a sheer volume of money. Therefore previously, sender(s) need to save reasonable wealth. In long-run, expenditures would follow certain trend so that Government can design a plan to provide their expense, also a part of expenditure can provide by making policy and giving political points.

-**Target** : Cutting relationship between Target and other countries lead to a decrease in income but countries have short-run and long-run planning so that expected income can reflect in budget. On the other hand each country has various public welfare plans like Subsidies which contain considerable costs. An decrease in income can cripple Government, but authority use the stack of wealth to continue its duties. It can be argued that the reduction of wealth can affect on social services so that people cannot bear these conditions and Target capitulate to Sender(s).

-**Example** : Libya just after two years from the declaration of 731 in 1992, due to unsuitable condition and the shortage of sources, conditionally accepted to have cooperation with Security council but there was opposition so that Sanctions had continued until 2003 which the president of Libya accepted all requisitions of Western countries.

2.2.3 Social & Religious Structure

a) Religion

Religion is a main factor which affect the percipience of society and reaction to sanctions because in the majority of countries (with democratic structure), people is considered as an essential element. Authority would encounter with special circumstances like Sanction and tackle problems if people support their Government. Different religions have various priority about profit maximization and utility so that a series of religions protect the maximization of individual utility, conversely some religions protect social utility and third groups protect the moderate view between individual and social utility.

-Sender(s) : Authorities in order to impose Sanction on Target need the protection of people. Governments are not able to unveil the profits of Sanction for their people, hence the level of individualism in each country can specify the role of Government. It is clear that for achieving the protection of people in Sanction, Government can draw the individual expected utility for manipulating people. Conversely, Collectivism in some countries can help Government because an increase in patriotic feelings can absorb the protection of people.

-Target : Sanctions impose the onerous condition on Target and Government should spend the cost of individualism because each person has specific interests and the maximization of society depends on individuals. On the other hand Collectivism can curtail expenditures.

-**Example** : North Korea has thwarted Sanctions by Collectivism, whilst militarism and a harsh condition in this country play main role to continue this trend.

b) Historical experience

Societies learn of history and draw expected horizon, thus if a society has experienced bout Sanction as Target or Sender , success and defeat would affect societies' moral in new challenge.

-**Sender** : People in support of Government can play important role to achieve goals, therefore if a society win at the similar challenge and achieve the profit of Sanction, Government would have the protection of people in new Sanction.

-**Target** : Conquest in war can improve nationalism and Social morals but resistance to Sanction cannot persuade people to bear new challenges because it does not have clear profit in return for hard condition along a Sanction.

-**Example** : US throughout the history in order to advocate the interests, use Sanctions against many countries such as India, Afghanistan, Iraq, Libya, Haiti ,Iran and ... .But this the results of Sanction were not acceptable so that war was a solution to keep the prosperity. Correlation between defeats and protestations is clear in US.

c) *The power of publicity*

New world order has led to an increase in the supervision of international organization about any activity over the world. There is no doubt that nowadays each Challenges like Sanctions and its results affect all people over the world and Governments would follow people's interests.

-**Sender(s)** : Sanctions would be effective if other countries support Sender(s). On the other hand people in modern society play main role to make decision, so that Government should absorb people's view for cooperating with Sender(s). The power of publicity can persuade people to accept the policy of Government, in fact many countries pay considerable costs for broadening authorities' view.

-Target : Target can improve defensive structure by international mass media so that Target can entice a part of public voice to increase their pressure on Sender(s) for breaking Sanctions.

-Example : International protestations have increased after the function of Reporters Without Borders in Gaza therefore many countries have requested Israel to decrease the pressure of Sanctions.

2.3 Kinds of Sanctions

Sanctions is divided into two groups;

1. Pure Sanctions : Sender(s) impose Sanctions on Target in order to punishment.

2. Sanctions and Incentives : There are various incentives along with Sanctions which coerce Target into changing its behavior.

Sender(s) can use various combinations of Sanctions which contain pure Sanction or/and a series of incentives, but the usage of each method depends on conditions and a kind of violation.

It is necessary to survey different kinds of Sanctions over the history and each Sanction with the mentioned structure can encompass following ways.

2.3.1 Bans on Trade

This Sanction can attack the efficiency of Governments. The main purpose is to challenge Government because people following an increase in inflation would lose their Economic power, on the other hand Government cannot control the level of prices because other countries have ceased their Economic relations with Target, hence authority cannot import goods in order to an decrease in inflation. It is clear that at least in short-run Target would encounter with high inflation.

Exports can help Government acquiring money for purchasing goods, therefore after Sanctions, Exports decrease to the lowest level also the power of breaking Sanction would decrease severely. In addition for the sake of providing goods, Government should buy or sell goods in black markets.

This Sanction can include the trade of weapons because the majority of Sanctions to be finished by war, therefore a decline in the power of Target's military can be one of the most important aims of Sanctions. Military power of Target can be a cause of Sanctions, for example the aim of some Sanctions is to dismantle Target's WMD.

2.3.2 Bans on Finance

Unemployment in Sanctions condition is one of the factors of people protests which affect Government decisions. Therefore Sender(s) can affect foreign investment and indirectly decrease the level of employment. This condition means that Target lose one of the most important motivating tools for increasing the level of employment in Economy. Impose a ban on

Finance and Trade may result in Stagflation which is another economic disease.

Developed countries invest in developing countries to acquire cheap workers, in return these investments can help to surge efficiency and the level of employment. Therefore embargo can reduce the efficiency and employment in Target. on the other hand Government halt incomplete projects for the sake of insufficient finance. It is clear that new projects because of Scale & Scope, cannot optimize profits. Thus new occupation opportunity is not congruent with new unemployment labor force, also many Economic policy incline to a decrease in population.

2.3.3 Freezing of Assets

The assets of Target in foreign countries can help resisting in Sanction condition because embargo on trade lead to a decrease in foreign revenue, hence these assets can be helpful for purchasing needs from black markets. Obviously, freezing of assets can cripple Target by increasing the pressure upon government and people.

Many firms have Economic relations with Target in order to maximize their profits. Thus Sender(s) recognize companies and firms which break Sanctions, then Sender(s) retaliate against these Economic agencies by freezing of assets.

2.3.4 Bans on Cash Transfer

Some countries in order to acquire high benefits continue their economic ties with Target, on the other hand Sender(s) for the sake of increasing control on international markets would not reproach these countries. Sender(s) for increasing the pressure upon Target, Impose a ban on cash transfer and coerce banks into cutting economic relations with Target. These condition lead to barter exchange deals which can decrease the trade of weapons.

2.3.5 Bans on Technology Transfer

Scientific improvements can be seen in various technologies and each technology has ability to be used in various sectors, therefore if the aim of sanction is to reducing the pace of achieving specific goals, Sender(s) would impose a ban on special technologies transfer.

2.3.6 Restrictions on Travel

Smart Sanctions can affect special individuals in Government. Restrictions on travel is a kind of Sanctions which prevent some aims of Target in foreign countries by considering various barriers on the way of travelling, therefore experts of Target cannot travel to other countries for breaking Sanctions. It is clear that in the majority of cases, Restrictions on travel is a kind of admonishment.

2.4 Scale & Scope of Sanction

Politicians specify the aims of Sanctions and Economists should minimize the costs of Sanctions. Sanctions have various costs but The size of Sanction is the most important factor which can play main role in surging the costs, it means that a Sanction can be Smart or Comprehensive. On the other hand the number of countries which cooperate in Sanction, is so important in order to achieve goals.

2.4.1 Scope of Sanction

Diverse factors affect the scope of Sanctions. Majority of Sanctions impose pressure on Target gradually so that initially, Smart Sanctions influence special sectors in order to compel a change in Target behavior but unsuccessful Smart Sanction lead to a new level of Sanctions. This trend would be continued until sweeping measures against Target.

Sanctions work as Valve, therefore close the valve gradually can impose high pressure on Target. Different aspects result in gradual Sanctions, putting pressure upon people is considered as an immoral attitude by The public voice. On the other hand the comprehensive sanctions have different lateral effects on Economy of the world. Therefore if Target plays pivotal function in international ties, the results of Sanctions would decrease the supply of important goods. In addition Sender(s) should pay more costs in the comprehensive Sanctions for supervising The performance of Sanctions, but The dilemma is the cost of incentives, considering by Sender(s) in order to entice countries to joint rally.

2.4.2 Scale of Sanction

The scale of Sanctions shows cooperation of different countries with Sender(s) also the scale is affected by the scope of Sanctions. Generally, Sender(s) might be a special country, a groups of countries or Security Council, therefore Sanctions can be supported by different levels of power. An increase in the number of Senders would increase the power of supervision, thus Target cannot break Sanctions and the pressure upon Target would increase dramatically. Sender(s) persuade other countries to joint rally, although it does not mean that All of them have common interests because some countries joint Sender(s) in return for political advantages and Economic points.

2.5 Action & Reaction to Sanction (Use of Game Theory)

Totally, each Sanction has two sides which play strategic game, hence the best tool for analyzing the oppositeness is Game Theory. Here we would conduct the survey of action and reaction to Sanctions but we abstain from complicated analyzing.

2.5.1 Game of Strategy

The first assumption is that we have two choices for Target :

1. Target violate Sender's requisitions which is shown by "Violate"

2. Target comply with Sender's requisitions which is shown by "Comply"

The second assumption is that we have two choices for Sender :

1. The comprehensive Sanction which is shown by "Sanction"

2. Sender dispense with Sanction which is shown by "No Sanction"

Table 1, shows four results of Game

General Payoff Matrix of Sanctions Game

	Sanction	No Sanction
Violate	$a_1 \, a_2$	$b_1 \, b_2$
Comply	$c_1 \, c_2$	$d_1 \, d_2$

Assumptions : $b_1 > d_1$, $d_2 > c_2$, $c_1 > a_1$, and $a_2 > b_2$.

(Table 1)

A logic assumption is that in a condition with no Sanction, Target violate Sender's standard. Therefore we have :

ASSUMPTION 1: $b_1 > d_1$

On the other hand another logic assumption is that Sender should pay cost for imposing Sanction. Therefore in a condition that Target observes the rules, sender would not use Sanction. In mathematical model we have :

ASSUMPTION 2: $d_2 > c_2$

Also another assumption shows that the comprehensive Sanction can cease any violation of standards, thus Target prefer to renounce inflammatory actions.

ASSUMPTION 3: $c_1 > a_1$

It is clear that if Target violate standards, Sender would impose Sanction upon Target. Here we have Mathematical model :

ASSUMPTION 4: $a_2 > b_2$

For acquiring utility functions, it is necessary to assume that the action of players are simultaneously and both of them have sufficient information, in addition two players have logic behavior. Each player can determine the level of strategy (Target would select the level of x to violate and Sender would select the level of Y to Sanction). In a condition that Target choose perfect violation, x=1, conversely in a condition that Target comply with standard, x=0. There are similar assumptions for Sender so that in the condition of no Sanction, y=0, whilst in a comprehensive Sanction, y=1.

Now we would survey another assumption, payoffs of each player is a linear function from both players' strategies. Consequently, the utility function of each player is shown here :

$$u_1 = (d_1-c_1-b_1+a_1)xy + (c_1-d_1)y + (b_1-d_1)x + d_1 \quad (equ\ 1)$$

$$u_2 = (d_2-c_2-b_2+a_2)xy + (b_2-d_2)x + (c_2-d_2)y + d_2 \quad (equ\ 2)$$

Mentioned functions can be used in order to determine Nash equilibrium. Strategies equilibrium would be shown like a pair of strategy (x*,y*) which is the optimum response of players. In fact if players choose another pair of strategy, one of them would change the strategy and the second one in return of first player action would change strategy too.

Here we have the definition of Nash equilibrium for the Game of Sanction :

$$x^* = (d_2-c_2) / (d_2-c_2+a_2-b_2) \quad (equ\ 3)$$

$$y^* = (b_1-d_1) / (b_1-d_1+c_1-a_1) \quad (equ\ 4)$$

It is possible to show that the equilibrium has all terms which is necessary in Games Theory.

Changing in the terms of Game can reveal secrets of different conditions. For instance, one of the most important rules of Game Theory is logic players, while illogic players up to certain level can improve strategy because the Game would be unforeseeable.

2.5.2 Why imposing Sanction on Israel cannot be successful ?

One of the challenges in the world is Anti-Semitic among Muslims but Islamic countries have not imposed Sanction on Israel yet. It is possible to analyze the reasons of this condition by Game Theory.

Apart from a series of powerful Islamic countries which have close relationship with Israel and Sanction is against of their interests, other Islamic countries are hostile to Israel. Religious conditions have divided Islamic countries to different groups, For example Sunni and Shiite . Israel is more powerful than each Islamic country in terms of Economy and military. Therefore for the hegemony of Target, Islamic groups/countries have almost the same status against Israel.

-We assume that each Islamic group can choose two strategies:

1. Islamic countries sanction Israel which has benefit "V" and cost "C". Islamic groups would gain profit but it is clear that Israel would retaliate against these groups, therefore net benefit can be "V-C" :

$$V > C > 0 \quad (equ\ 5)$$

2. No Sanction, this condition leads to normal situation that cost and benefit are zero.

-We assume that the number of Islamic groups are "n".

-The probability of "Sanction" is "p" and the probability of "No Sanction" is "1-p", therefore we encounter with a symmetric Nash equilibrium :

$$1 > p > 0 \quad (equ\ 6)$$

Table 2 represents four various payoffs

General Payoff Matrix of Contribution Game

		(n-1) Groups	
		No Sanction	At Least One Group Sanctions
One Group	One Group Sanctions	V-C	V-C
	No Sanction	0	V

(Table 2)

We want to survey actions and reactions of Islamic groups against each other for imposing Sanction on Israel. Totally we have to choose a group from "n" groups, thus "n-1" groups remain that the probability of each one is "p" to use Sanction. Therefore the probability of "No Sanction" is $(1-p)^{n-1}$ and the probability of "At least one Sanction" is $1-(1-p)^{n-1}$.

A group which has been chosen would impose Sanction with the probability of "q" and the probability of "No Sanction" is 1-q. Nash equilibrium would be accessible if "p" be equal to "q" .

Selected group has the best response function as below :

(Expected Profit) $\pi_1 = q.(V - C) + (1-q)(0 + V(1-(1-p)^{n-1}))$ *(equ 7)*

if $V - C > V(1-(1-p)^{n-1})$, $q = 1 \implies$ **MAX** π_1 *(equ 8)*

if $V - C < V(1-(1-p)^{n-1})$, $q = 0 \implies$ **MAX** π_1 *(equ 9)*

if $V - C = V(1-(1-p)^{n-1})$, $q \in [0, 1) \implies$ *Indifference Terms* *(equ 10)*

Symmetry term cannot be obtained when "q=1" or "q=0", because of "p ≠ q" (previously, we showed that 1>p>0).

third condition can show Symmetry term that "p=q", therefore below equation result in Nash equilibrium :

$C / V = (1 - p)^{n-1} \implies p = 1 - (C / V)^{1/n-1}$ *(equ 11)*

Here, Nash equilibrium can introduce one of the interesting problems in sociology. Increasing in the number of Islamic countries "n", would decrease the probability of Sanction because Islamic countries do not have enough cooperation.

Each group in order to prevent any retaliation would wait for other groups action. therefore when the number of countries be increased without powerful leader, the effect of Israel behavior would be divided into Islamic groups. All groups prefer to achieve "V" unit of profit without cost because among considerable Islamic countries, they reckon that their action would not be under vision of other countries.

There are many cases that a series of countries with common interests impose Sanctions on Target, but the mentioned problems would not be serious. For example European Union use Sanction for punishing Russia about an invasion of Ukraine in 2013.European countries have common interests so that border is not obstacle for relations between countries, on the other hand powerful integration among countries has led to a political power.

2.6 The Reaction of Target against World

Sanction is a kind of cold war. the qualification of countries for victory in this condition depends on various parameters. Countries enter the Game of strategies and each country which has powerful tools, can achieve goals with high probability. Nowadays, impressing the societies of the world and acquiring more protection can be more effective than other weapons. Two sides of Sanction can change the condition to advocate the interests by victory at this front. Diverse factors play role in order to achieve this aim, thus Sender(s) would analyze these elements before any actions. It is clear that Sender(s) would consider suitable strategy for decreasing the sensitiveness of world society.

The power of military, economic, policy and media are four elements which can affect the approaches of bilateral countries and Sender(s).

2.6.1 Power of Target's Army

Military power is a kind of tool which can be used by Target as the last chance against Sender(s), but normal military power (in comparison with WMD) cannot act as a deterrent factor. On the other hand the majority of Sender(s) have considerable military power, therefore normal military power would not be a threat for world security.

Nuclear and chemical weapons are the red lines of world society, while these kind of weapons can work as deterrent tools against war and Sanctions. Imposing Sanction on nuclear countries would encounter with high risk reactions, therefore Sender(s) should have powerful army and powerful Sanction tools although Target would not use nuclear weapons.

The cost of Sender(s) would increase dramatically if Target has military power in neighbors. These military groups can be considered as potential threat for Sender(s) because Sender(s) have many interests around Target thus Sanction can entice Target to hurt these accessible interests. Therefore the interests of Sender(s) in related district should be determined before any actions. Increasing the power of defense against military groups, would surge the amount of costs.

The size of Sanction is the most important factor which can change in behavior of Target. Obviously, the probability of war would increase if the comprehensive Sanction be considered by Sender(s), hence Sender(s) can regularize the size of Sanction for preventing war.

2.6.2 Power of Target's Economy

Advocating the economic interests means to save social welfare, therefore Target can protect its authority and acquire some scores by imperiling Sender's interests. Sender(s) should analyze the potential of Target which can threat world society. Generally, Target can affect other countries in three way, although the intenseness of reaction depends on the size of Sanction because in rational condition, there is a proportion between action and reaction.

- **Slashing imports of Sender(s) and their united :** The first reaction of Target can be cutting economic ties with Sender(s) and increasing the consolidation of economic relation with bilateral countries. This condition can impose pressure upon Sender(s) and replace them by new partners which can be helpful in hard situation. This possible reaction should be considered by leader of Sender(s) and proposes suitable country for superseding. In some cases before any Sanctions, Senders(s) decrease imports of Target and try to replace Target with new country so that Target in Sanction condition would not increase pressure upon Sender(s), whilst this policy can be a convenient signal for forecasting Sanction.

- **Target has the sources of energy and primary goods :** All industrial countries by using two factors can produce goods which are energy and primary goods. In the scarce of these factors, the cost of producing and the level of price would be increased thus demand would be decreased, on the other hand it would have unexpected results by terms of the elasticity of market. the country which have a sheer volume of resources of primary goods and energy, can affect the level of general price over the world by regulating exports. This advantage can work as disadvantage because the countries with considerable resources in order to continuing their existence depend on the exports of raw material. Therefore comparative Sanction can make Sender(s) to pay more cost in return of imposing a ban on the exports of raw materials. This condition can damage the economic structure of Target and on the other hand can increase the profit of other countries which export raw materials.

-**Strategic territory** : the countries which located in transit area can block the transit way in order to a disturbance in world economy order. Therefore changing the ways of international transportation can surge the cost of final goods and this condition would damage other countries' economy. Forecasting the critical condition by Sender(s) would affect strategies, because the security of main transit ways is the most important lateral effect of Sanctions. At the most of time Sender(s) use their military power to save the security of goods transportation throughout the world.

2.6.3 Power of Target's Diplomacy

Diplomacy at the high level and Lobbying in other countries can force allies to join a rally against Sender(s) which can increase the cost of continuing Sanctions. It is clear that if supporter of Target has had chair in security council, Target would gain considerable scores. Generally, policy can achieve Target to its aims through three ways :

- **Experienced Diplomats :** Each international complicated challenge needs tortuous negotiations and Diplomacy sector of each country would shows its efficiency at these situations. Many Sanctions come to an end with hard negotiations but it is of importance that Target has valuable tools for increasing the pressures upon Sender(s) in order to supporting diplomats .

- **Political power and Lobbying in neighbors :** Imposing ban on export and import lead to hard condition in Target, therefore authority would use political relations with neighbors in order to breaking Sanctions. Vast amount of goods can import of neighbors illegally.

- **Political power in the world :** Many countries have ideological proponents among people over the world, hence people put pressure upon Governments to protect Target and a new rally would be formed against Sender(s) which can increase the cost of Sanctions. On the other hand the thought of West and East bloc can be helpful for Target, because powerful countries in Security council would help their proponent against opposite bloc . Thus the reasonable relation with the members of international organization would be wisely decision for advocating the interests.

2.6.4 Power of Target's Media

Nowadays after scientific improvement in the field of media, the public voice have acted as an important factor in foreign policy. Obviously, an increase in a pace of information transfer which issue huge amount of news without editing over the world, would affect people's emotions and Governments should be responsible to people's requisitions.

Political challenge between Sender(s) and Target lead to new front which each side try to absorb the public voice, hence Target's media can issue Sanction news one sided and evoke public emotions throughout the world.

It is clear that at the majority of cases these medias would not show the facts.

2.7 Using Sanction

At this level Sender(s) imposing Sanctions upon Target. By considering the violation of standards behaviors, Sender(s) would coerce Target into changing its approaches by using Sanctions. Therefore it is necessary to study the structure of Target and forecasting the probability of damages that other countries may encounter with. Thus a simulation by Games Theory can show the effects of Sanctions on the word and Target. The results of primary measures should be derived quantitatively also the costs of Sanctions as well as its profit should be determined. Therefore once the costs are more than benefits, Sender(s) would not use comprehensive Sanctions although they can retaliate against Target by Smart Sanctions.

2.8 Review & Error Correction

The results of Sanctions would be surveyed by experts periodically but at the majority of periods the results would not be acceptable because Sanction is dynamic action. Therefore the scope of Sanctions as well as the goals of sender(s) would be revised and new Sanctions would be used to achieve goals. Forecasting the reactions of Target would be so hard if Target's functions be illogical. However illogical functions in Sanction condition can warrant the chance of survival. When Sender(s) use Sanctions by considering the reaction of Target, behavior models should be drawn which can be helpful for reviewing strategies and error corrections. the next stage is new Sanction which impose more pressure upon Target.

2.9 The Last Decision

Sanctions can have various results by considering the structure of Target. Sanctions in terms of period and size can have high or low intensity, therefore if Sanctions lead to positive results for Sender(s), would be hopeful to continue the trend. It seems that war would be the last solution if Target be insistent for violating of standards. Obviously, when Target has considerable military power, war would be replaced by win- win negotiation.

Economic Aspects of Sanction

1. Costs & Benefits of Sender(s)

Introduction

Sanction is a kind of investment that Sender(s) should pay costs for acquiring profits in future. Therefore the costs and benefits of Sanction should be determined . In this capture we want to describe the economic aspects of Sanctions and show that the sanction can be a losing Game for both sides.

1.1 Commercial & Monetary Ties Changing

Sender(s) should pay considerable costs for limiting Target and cutting the access of Target to international Trade and fiscal markets. For persuading other countries to join rally, Sender(s) should recommend new markets, with the same interests instead of Target, to their allies. Another assumption is that Sender(s) by reducing their tariffs, try to save the interests of allies in Sanctions. However many countries for enticing other, use political concessions instead of Economic incentives.

Freezing assets and imposing bans on cash transfer in bilateral countries would be possible if Sender propose interesting concessions to Banks. On the other hand fiscal Sanctions should be backed by international organizations such as Security council. Cutting the cooperation between Target and Foreign Banks means that the credit of Target as well as foreign income would decrease in the world. Therefore Sender(s) would pay costs for achieving this aim, whilst if the amount of money which circulate between these Banks and Sender be considerable, the Banks would not violate the requisition of Sender.

Generally, Trade and Fiscal Sanctions change the behavior models of some economic agencies, hence many long-run Trade contrasts would not able to continue. The process of finding new Trade partner instead of Target may take long time which can damage the Economy of Senders and many people would lose their jobs. Therefore the leader of Sanctions should find reasonable solution and provide incentives to entice other countries for saving integration.

1.2 Losing Market

Imposing embargo on Trade means that Sender(s) would lose the markets of Target. It can be assumed that foreign agencies which work in Target are logical and efficient, thus the markets of Target should be the best choice for these foreign agencies among other countries. It seems that these markets would be considered as opportunity cost. Before Sanctions, the broadening of Trade between Target and Sender(s) is an important factor for declaring about superseding markets.

Reciprocal demand curves show the level of exports and imports at various level of prices for different countries. these curves would represent the facts that Sanctions can affect Trade and social welfare.

Initial offer curve in Figure 1, denotes the equilibrium between a country with a potential for being Target (offer curve T) and Trade partners which include other countries (offer curve W).

Horizontal axis shows the amount of export by a country called T (XT) and vertical axis shows the amount of import by T (MT). Each point along offer curve T, represents a special equilibrium for T in international trade so that the proportion of import price to export price would declare the slope of this curve.

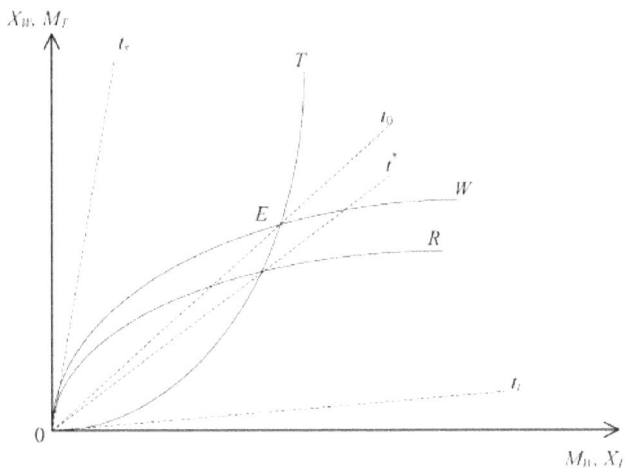

(*Fig. 1*)

Also this Figure denotes the combination of other countries offer curves (W). We assume that other countries export a good which is imported by Target, therefore vertical axis shows MT and XW. Other countries would import a good which is exported by Target then XT and MW is shown by horizontal curve. Here we have simple assumption, showing that Target is only supplier of XT thus has comparative advantage against other countries for producing this good. Intersection E, between two offer curves W and T shows an international Trade equilibrium. This intersection shows the equilibrium that is located on the line t_0 and this line represents the equality between supply & demand simultaneously.

Now assume that other countries (W) impose the comprehensive Sanctions upon (T). This Sanction forces Target to move from trade equilibrium (E) to autarky (0) by annihilating the trade opportunity between W and T. Sanction would worsen the situation if trade condition moves from t_0 to t_t. This Figure declare that the costs of Sanction can hurt Senders in addition to Target because Senders would choose the autarky condition consciously and trade condition transfers to t_s. This movement from trade equilibrium would damage the welfare of Senders like the movement of Target from t_0 to t_s which increases net price of import.

The amount of movement from given conditions depends on the curvature of offer curve which is function of the price-elasticity of the offer to trade and the size of the trading countries. When a big country enters trade relations, the size of its Economy depends on the amount of trade that it undertakes ensures that the equilibrium terms of trade cannot be very different from the autarky terms of trade. Very large countries are self-sufficient enough to not reap very substantial gains from trade, but conversely they do not suffer extensively from abstaining from trade, following sanctions. Thus large-country offer curves have very little curvature, almost resembling linear rays from the origin. Small countries, however, tend to be much more dependent on trade. Their demands for and supplies of tradable goods are price-inelastic and these countries can suffer greatly from the imposition of sanctions. Thus, small countries tend to have much more curvature in their offer curves than do large countries.

Let us now consider the economic effects of unilateral sanctions on the target country and on the rest of the world. With the imposition of sanctions by one sanctioning country, S, the rest of the world's offer to trade with the target is reduced to the new offer curve, R, in Figure 1, since the sanctioning country's offer is removed from W at each terms of trade. The elasticity of this residual offer curve is also reduced by the sanctioning country's withdrawal, meaning that the new offer curve, R, must have a greater degree of curvature than the original offer curve, W. The opportunity to continue trading with those nations that are not participating in the sanctions, however, means that the target country is not reduced to autarky as it was in the first example. Rather, trade continues for the target at somewhat worsened terms of trade, t^*, where the degree of deterioration in the target's terms of trade depends on the magnitude of the shift from W to R, and on the trade elasticity's involved. The greater the share of the target's presumptions trade accounted for by the sanctioning countries, or the larger the number of sanctioning countries relative to non-sanctimonies, the greater is the magnitude of the shift from W to R. As the number of sanctioning countries increases, we approach the multilateral case, with the target's terms of trade, t^*, approaching the autarky terms of trade, t_t . The less elastic is the rest-of-the-world offer curve, R, the greater the extent of the deterioration of the target's terms of trade. Although not shown explicitly in Figure 1, the deterioration of the target's terms of trade is also larger the more inelastic the target's offer curve.

1.3 Revenge
Sanctions can challenge the authority of Target, therefore if Target has comparative advantage of special good, Target would retaliate against Sender(s) by similar Sanctions. It is clear that Target can put the considerable costs on Sender(s). For instance, the countries which export energies like oil, can damage the structure of industrial countries although retaliated

Sanctions can annihilate the Economy of Target for the sake of Rentier State in these kind of countries.

Sender(s) would not use comprehensive Sanctions if the probability of retaliated Sanctions be estimated. Obviously, Sender(s) would impose Smart Sanctions like ban on travelling just for denoting dissatisfactions. However there is a probability of radical action like war which can advocate the interests of Sender(s) in short-run. Making decision at this condition would save public interests if Sender(s) utilize acceptable strategies.

1.4 Target Attitudes Changing

Sanction is a kind of political decision and has specific political interests, Sender(s) would use Sanction(s) in order to follow their policy over the world or secluding adversaries although the majority of political aims encompass Economic interests. . For example, the access to Economic sources by supporting specific party or changing political relations.

Changing the policy means that Target would accepts Sender(s) standard which include many economic concessions, therefore trade condition among countries would be accessible. Figure 2, represents details regarding the effect of changing policy on Sender's Economic condition. It means that the Economic thought of Sanctions can be result of inclination for increasing trade relations.

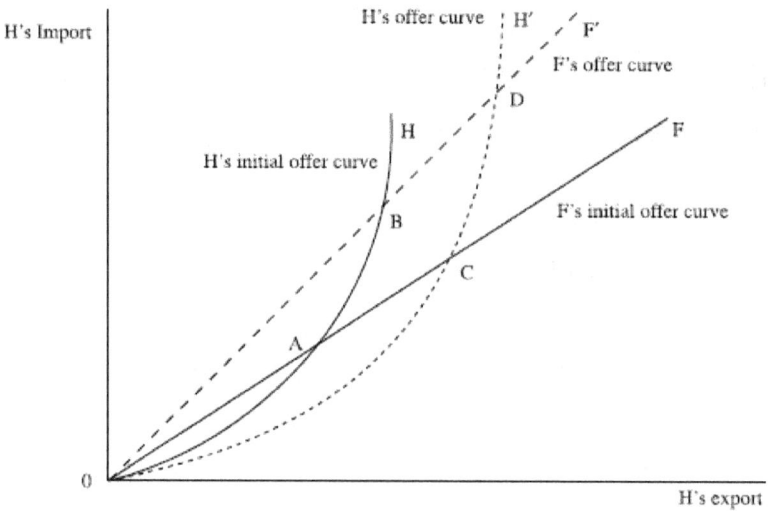

(Fig. 2)

Consider a two-country world in which small home country H (as Target), through reciprocal trade negotiations, negotiates the elimination of its own tariffs and those of partner F(as Sender), a country large enough to determine terms of trade. Because F now gives the small country H the advantage of trading with it for the first time at large country F's domestic terms of trade, H's terms of trade improve, i.e., its exporters escape from their past tariff payments to F's treasury. To illustrate in Figure 2, large foreign country F has a linear offer curve 0F: home country H cannot affect its terms of trade by unilaterally changing its tariff. (Its tariff reduction moves it from A to C.) However, if F is persuaded to also cut its tariff as part of a reciprocal deal, F's linear offer curve will rotate to 0F', and equilibrium shifts to D where H's terms of trade have improved. In short, in a reciprocal negotiation, a small country with no unilateral terms-of-trade influence can do something it cannot do on its own: improve its terms of trade. It does so by persuading its new large partner, whose barriers do affect the terms of trade, to reduce its tariff; i.e., on the exports of H, F offers price-taking H a better price to take. But why would large country F be willing to participate in an agreement that, by cutting its tariff, would damage its terms of trade? The answer may be either foreign policy or other non-economic reasons; or economic reasons already noted such as H's agreement to reform its treatment of foreign investment or intellectual property. Or F may benefit economically because, in an n-country world, it is negotiating for mutual gain with other large third countries (with small country H acquiring a terms-of-trade benefit as a side effect). Alternatively in an reciprocal trade negotiations, F may have an economic incentive to reduce its tariff because domestic political pressures have raised it substantially above its optimal level.

To sum up: the assumption that the home country is small that has been used to freeze its terms of trade under unilateral tariff reduction and thus guarantee it against a loss, also ensures it a terms-of-trade gain from reciprocal trade negotiations in which large partners reduce their tariffs. Thus even a small country – indeed, especially a small country – cannot compare these two policies without recognizing that reciprocity can be expected to provide better terms of trade than unilateral tariff reduction, because reciprocity reduces foreign tariffs. This is another illustration of the theoretical damage done in any analysis of reciprocal trade negotiations that is preoccupied only with own-tariff removal and thus overlooks foreign tariff reduction.

1.5 Supply Domination

Imposing an embargo upon a country can cut the export of Target therefore if Target has considerable proportion of international trade of specific good and on the other hand Sender(s) produce this kind of good, what would be happened after a dramatic decrease in the supply of the good ?

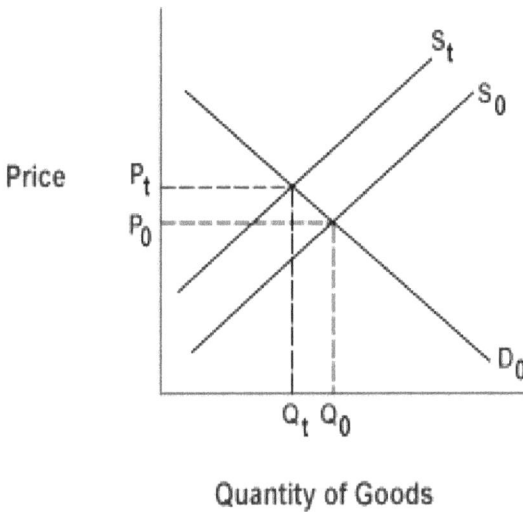

(Fig. 3)

Generally, this condition would have two main effects that are kind of rent for Sender(s). By considering Figure 3, assume that Target & Sender are two main steel supplier thus the intersection of demand (D_0) and supply (S_0) can determine the equilibrium of market but after using Sanction against one of the main steel supplier, supply line (S_0) will shift to left and new equilibrium would be constituted by last demand (D_0). An increase in the level of price from P0 to Pt by considering the kind of market and the slop of demand line can provide considerable profit for Sender(s).

The issue can be argued from other view, Increasing the price of primary goods means that the variable costs of production would surge and consequently final price of goods increase dramatically. Increasing the price of steel would challenges various industrial sectors and lead to an increase in the level of industrial goods price. Hence producer throughout the world by considering the elasticity of market would sustain a loss after increasing the price, therefore Sender(s) with the main proportion of steel market can be a price maker and improve national industry with the new rents, also Sender(s) can kick rivals out of market.

Sometimes the scarce of steel can cause unbelievable damages so that Sender(s) would not able to compensate for this scarce. Therefore Sender(s) would allow Target to export its good for controlling the level of price over the world, this action is so-called Valve controlling that Target and other countries would acquiring new profits.

1.6 Increasing Risk

Imposing an embargo upon a country that is one of the main supplier of strategic goods results in serious price fluctuations because increasing uncertainly about the shortage of goods, also surges the risk of investments in essential and complementary industries. On the other hand some economic unjustifiable projects which can produce substitute goods, after Sanctions would be justifiable.

Assume that, after using Sanctions against an oil reach country, uncertainly about energy supply increase. Therefore prices have severe fluctuations and increasing the price of oil by considering the constancy of other conditions, would decrease the demand of heavy cars also it would encompass normal cars if uncertainly increases in society. It is clear that various industries would damage if the demand of car decrease significantly therefore the number of unemployment would increase sharply.

Investment in this sector has considerable risk because the price fluctuation of oil and gas is unpreventable, hence substitute goods which were not justifiable, would be low risk projects such as electrical battery. Sender(s) can use this condition and information for improving the production of substitute goods which contain high profits with low risk.

2. The Cost of Target

Introduction

Trade in proportion to GDP (Gross Domestic Product) shows Economic openness which can determine the volume of Sanction effectiveness. Initially, we should survey the main sectors of Economy for costs assessment.

In Figure 4, we can see various sectors of each Economy that generally, there are seven macro sectors and many sub-sectors. Economic Sanctions can affect all parts of each country through foreign sector in order to achieve specific aims. Therefore countries which have considerable international economic ties would be more vulnerable than close countries against Sanctions. Whether this fact means that close Economies have more advantages than open Economies ?

Certainly no, a country with close Economy did not acquire the interests of trade with other countries in the period before Sanctions. Obviously, if Senders find that their Sanctions are not able to work as a deterrent tool, they would use substitute tools which can be military actions.

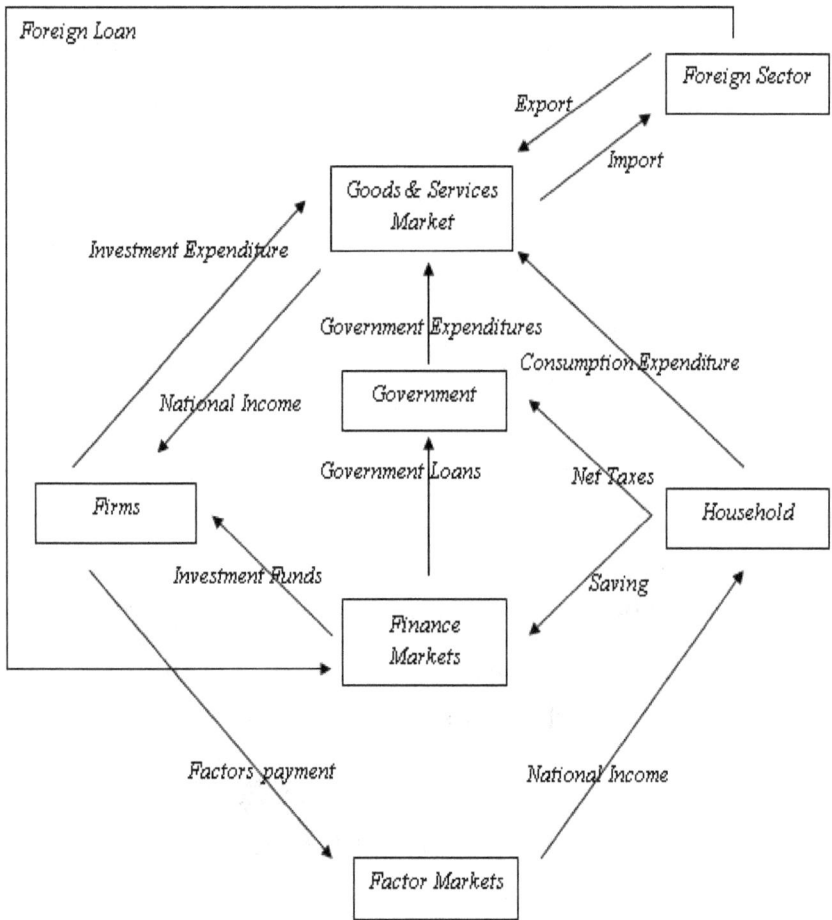

(Fig. 4)

However open Economies have engaged in strengthening infrastructures by using the interests of trade before Sanctions. The deference between open and close Economies in Sanctions condition return to social welfare. Close Economies would have $(X+3)/2$ units of welfare after Sanctions if they had $X+3$ units of welfare before that, on the other hand open Economies with $(X+3)^2$ units welfare would gain $(X+3)^2/2$ units after Sanctions.(Example was for broadening understanding)

Primary and simple societies which do not have complicated Economic ties would be less vulnerable than modern societies because in Economies with high interdependency if they have problem with Factor market, these difficulties would spread in other sectors. Hence this situation would be happen in Sanctions condition so that by imposing a ban on foreign sector, all other Economic sectors would be under pressure.

The relations among Economic sectors are not determined in primary societies, therefore the effectiveness of Sanctions cannot extend to other sectors. Thus is there any advantages for primary societies ?

Figure 4 just shows the relations among essential Economic sectors and monetary flow. Economic

Sanctions by disturbing export & import, transportation, trade, money transfer and finance can freeze Target Economy.

2.1 Disordering in Economic Growth

If Sender(s) use Sanctions for long time, the Economic Growth would encounter with many difficulties and Government is not able to save its tax income, therefore this factor lead to the decrease of Government expenditure (Government expenditure encompass consumption expenditure and investment expenditure). It is clear that Government would decline the expenditure but consumption expenditure cannot decrease dramatically because it has many employees but investment expenditure would curtail considerably and fiscal policies lose the efficiency. Hence Government would not able to expand infrastructures.

The countries which do not have suitable infrastructure for Economic development, would lose its dynamic also the cost of production would increase significantly. For instance, in Sanction condition, Government would not able to reconstruct energy transport systems which can lead to waste of energy and decreasing the efficiency of related firms, another example is about flaw in electronic infrastructure which can increase bureaucracy and the cost of production. One of the main reason for surging structural inflation is unsuitable infrastructure for facilitating trade. Now we survey the reasons of a decrease in national income and tax income.

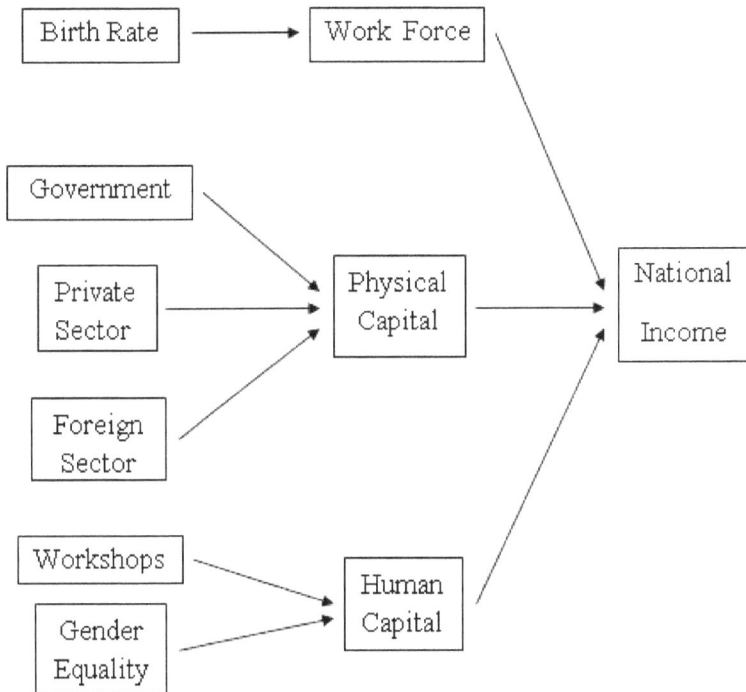

(Fig. 5)

Economist have designed various Economic Growth Models and we want to use endogenous income model in order to survey the effect of Sanctions on Growth.

$$Y=AK^{\alpha}L^{\beta}H^{\varphi} \qquad (equ\ 12)$$

As you see, National Income (Y) is dependent variable and independent variable are : Technology factor (A), Physical capital (K), Labor force (L) and Human capital (H). It is clear that the differential of Income proportion to basis year shows Economic Growth.

2.1.1 Labor Force

The Sanctions would make condition so difficult for households therefore birth rate would decrease dramatically but sanctions would affect labor market at least 15 years later (in short-run it does not have significant effect on the number of workers), on the other hand production in Sanction condition is not at the level of full employment thus the variation of labor force cannot influence National Income significantly.

2.1.2 *Physical Capital*

Government by using the superiority of information in Economy can choose high efficient investment and improve the aims of macroeconomics.

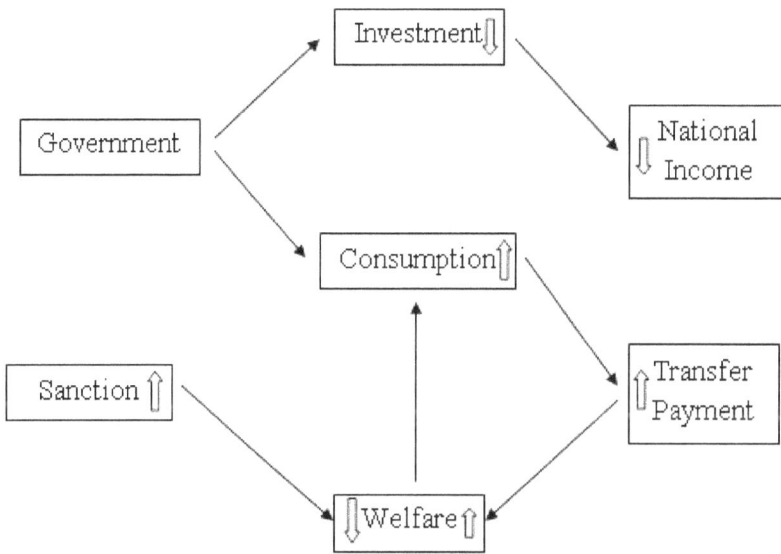

(Fig. 6)

Governments at the majority of time Invest in expanding infrastructures, therefore in Sanction condition, Government should increase the consumption expenditure for supporting society and it means that the investment expenditure would decrease and firms would not able to arrive the maximum of efficiency because Government cannot set the stage for Economic activities.

Privet sector has more efficient and effective investment in comparison with Government and Sanctions can affect investments through interest rate and uncertainty.

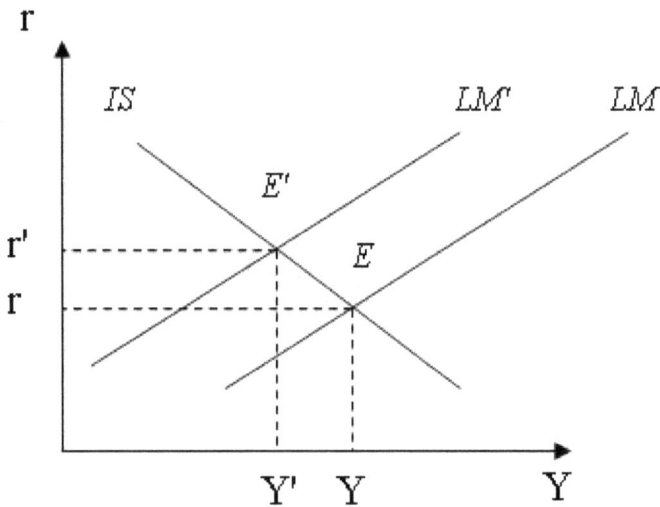

(Fig. 7)

After increasing uncertainty, liquidity preference would change hence monetary market encounters with new condition which LM curve would shifts to the left and the point E would transfers to the point E'. Therefore by increasing r to r', the amount of investment would decrease also production would follow it and experiences a dramatic decrease.

IS curve would experiences new condition after Sanctions. By regarding to below functions we would survey the effects of Sanctions on IS curve:

$$Y = C + I + G \qquad (equ\ 13)$$

$$C = a_0 - b\ (\ T_0 - TR_0\ ) + b\ (\ 1 - t\ )\ Y \qquad (equ\ 14)$$

$$I = I_0 - dr \qquad (equ\ 15)$$

$$G = G_0 \qquad (equ\ 16)$$

$$A_0 = a_0 - b\ (T_0 - TR_0\ ) + I_0 + G_0 \qquad (equ\ 17)$$

$$Y = \frac{1}{1-b\ (1-t)}\ (\ A_0 - dr\ ) \qquad (equ\ 18)$$

And finally we would have in terms of r :

$$r = \frac{A_0}{d} - \frac{Y}{d.k} \qquad (equ\ 19)$$

As you seen, an intercept depends on independent consumptions, therefore because Sanction decrease independent consumptions, it can be assumed that IS curve shifts to the left and interest rate as well as production would decrease (the slope of curve is effectiveness in the changes of interest rate and income) thus by regarding to the constancy of other conditions, Economic Growth would experience a significant decrease.

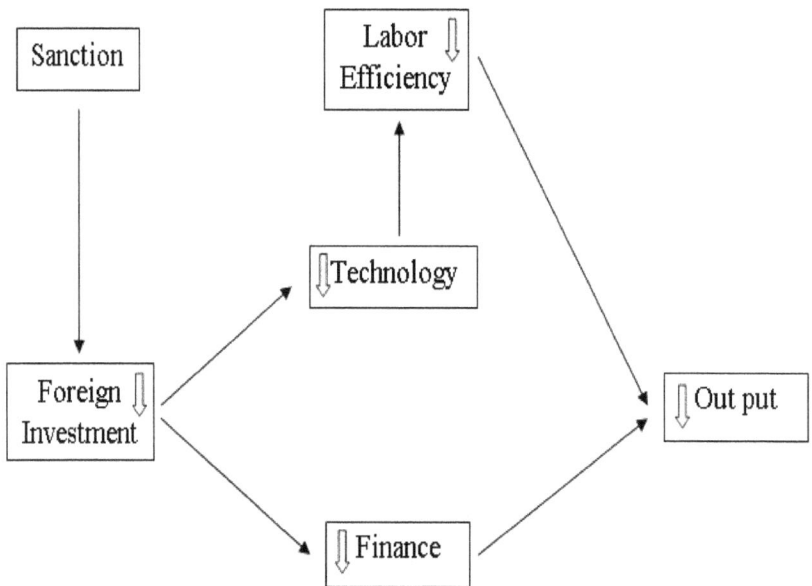

(Fig. 8)

In many high yield projects countries need high technologies and foreign exchange, therefore countries utilize foreign investors abilities to achieve their aims also foreign investment is a main tool for decreasing the gap between saving and domestic investment. Figure 8 denotes that Sanction is a factor for preventing the injection of foreign capital and high technologies to domestic production flow.

Foreign investment has considerable effects on Economy :

a) *Improving the efficiency of market:* Foreign investors need clear and complete information from markets in order to provide their expected profit, therefore for absorbing foreign investments, countries are bound to increase their efficiency.

b) *Increasing the liquidity of market:* Foreign capital with entry to monetary market results in an increase in liquidity and this happen would persuade other investors to start activity in market.

c) *Providing competitive atmosphere:* Foreign investments have economic goals, hence monopolization should be changed and this condition can surge the social welfare.

By regarding to mentioned terms, if Sender(s) impose a ban on finance, Target would lose many chances and National Income.

2.1.3 Human Capital

Labor teaching is the main factor for increasing efficiency thus in a Dynamic Economy in order to curtail the costs of production, should be increased the experience and knowledge of labor force. This aim in Sanction condition would not accessible completely because Sender(s) would not permit to transfer new knowledge from modern countries to Target.

Gender equality is a factor which Target can use for increasing human capital because women have hidden talents thus they would improve the efficiency of labor force if gender gap be decreased considerably.

2.2 Disordering in Goods & Services Market

Heart of each Economy is markets and social welfare depends on this sector, therefore imposing pressure upon market can disable authorities.

Imposing embargo on trade leads to a decrease in export & import.

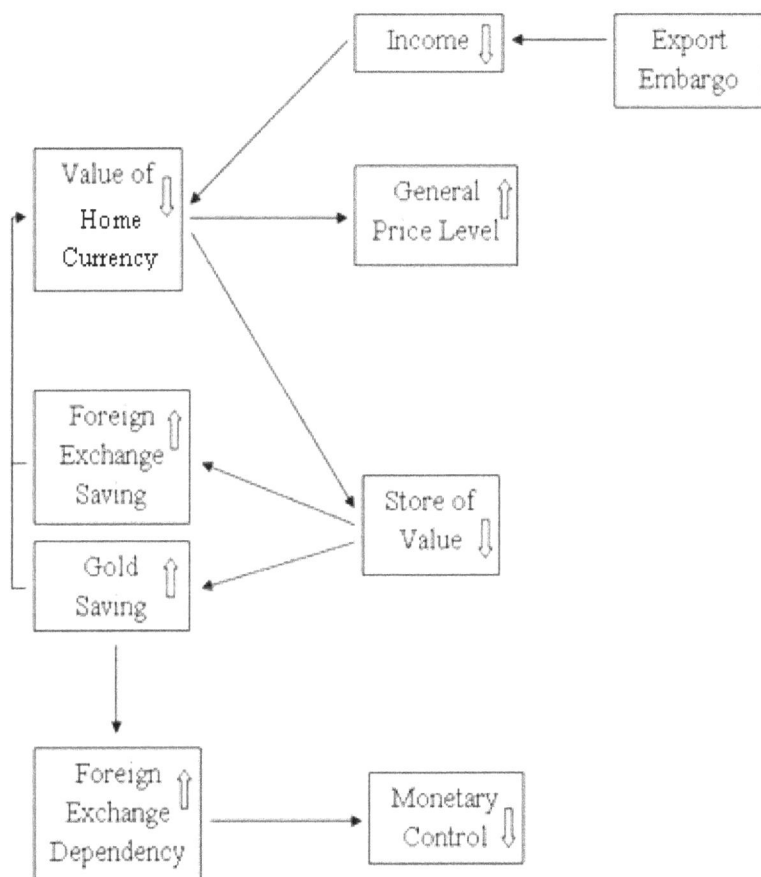

(Fig. 9)

A decline in foreign exchange income is one of the result of Imposing a ban on export, hence a decrease in foreign exchange supply would leads to an increase in the value of foreign exchange in comparison with home currency thus for purchasing a commodity, people should pay more than before and there is no doubt that an inflation would increase sharply.

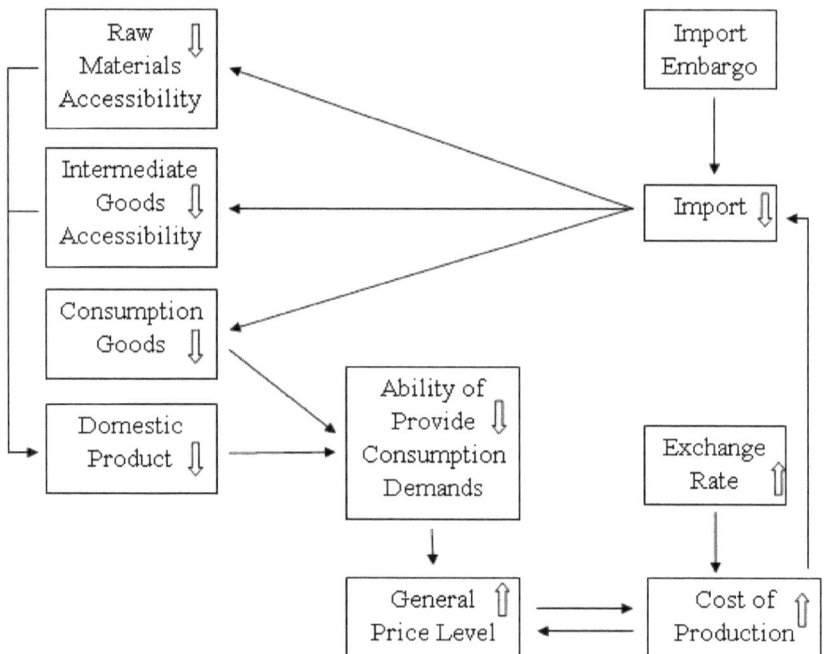

(Fig. 10)

On the other hand one of the main duty of money is saving the value so that it would decrease after declining the value of home currency, therefore people incline to save foreign currency and gold thus monetary controlling would decrease and production would be replaced by mediation thanks to high expected profit.

Imposing an embargo on import would disturb markets because the shortage of primary materials and intermediate goods can halt the process of production. A decrease in accessible to foreign consumption goods and declining the production result in market inefficiency for providing necessary provisions. Excess demand leads to an increase in inflation.

2.3 Disordering in Fiscal Market

2.3.1 Blocking Banks & Economic Systems

a) After Sanctions, considerable part of bank's sources in other countries would be endangered. Some foreign traders would encounter with various difficulties and the costs of trade increase dramatically.

b) Sanctions can make various obstacles in front of foreign currency sources so that traders who want to expand credit would encounter with many problems. On the other hand production depends on National and foreign currency thus this condition can delay contrast deadline. Therefore producers would be insolvency and in short time the claims of banks would not be payable although in long time the trend of claims would decrease because the expansion of LC decline gradually.

c) After Sanctions, there would be a doubt about the security of exports and the risk of intercourse with target would increase sharply, hence the rate of insurance would increases. All these reasons are enough for surging the final price of imports.

d) A decrease in the trust of foreign firms about Target's banks may result in cutting intercourse which can cause unexpected results.

e) a decline in public trust about banks can increase the probability of investment withdrawal, which can decrease the national production.

2.3.2 *Blocking Banks & Firms*

a) Mental effects of Sanctions on stock market would increase uncertainty among stockholders therefore they would sell their stocks so that the price of stocks decrease significantly. Firms use their stocks for hypothecating in banks, hence if the value of stocks drop considerably, banks would not able to use these pledges for their claims.

b) Ordinarily, for importing customers utilize LC and banks should expand LC. Sanctions disturb this condition and banks would not able to expand LC thus the economy of Target would be damaged. Firms import their primary materials through various connectors therefore final price of goods would increase sharply.

2.4 Disordering in Government Activities

The main purpose of each Sanction is to make Government inefficient, therefore decreasing the ability of monetary and fiscal policies can be helpful in this way. Second and third waves of Sanctions effects can damage tools which can help these policies. Imposing Sanctions on fiscal and goods market can show its effects in short time so that some indexes such as inflation, stagnation and unemployment that are symptoms in each Economy result in Government interference. Government after Sanctions wants to prevent the consequences hence some difficulties like high inflation and high unemployment can be foreseeable but the exact estimations would not be accessible. Government by using their estimations would utilize fiscal and monetary policies thus their actions can be self-destructor. On the other hand Sanctions can decline the public trust which may vary many parameters like marginal propensity to save and consume, therefore Government would not be able to use past information for the sake of Economic policies.

2.4.1 Fiscal Policy Efficiency

IS-LM model can show inefficiency of fiscal policy in Sanction condition.

As you see in Figure 11, in countries with high uncertainty the elasticity of money demand with regard to interest rate is low and this means that Crowding out is at high level. An increase in Government independent expenditure would lead to a decrease in private investment because interest rate has inverse relation with the level of investment.

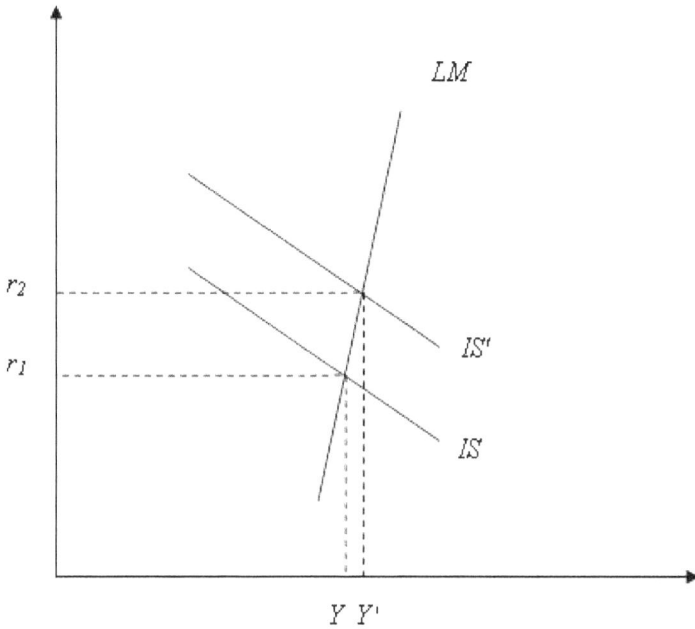

(*Fig. 11*)

Uncertainty is one of the most important factor which can increase risk in society.

$$Y = k (A_0 - dr)$$ (*equ 20*)

LM Function $$r = \frac{1}{h} (\alpha Y - \frac{MS_0}{P_0})$$ (*equ 21*)

$$Y = k \left[A_0 - \frac{d}{h} \left(\alpha Y - \frac{MS_0}{P_0} \right) \right] \qquad (equ\ 22)$$

$$Y = \frac{h \cdot k}{h + \alpha \cdot d \cdot k} \cdot A_0 + \frac{d \cdot k}{h + \alpha \cdot d \cdot k} \cdot \frac{MS_0}{P_0} \qquad (equ\ 23)$$

Fiscal policy multiplier $\quad \dfrac{\Delta Y}{\Delta A_0} = \dfrac{h \cdot k}{h + \alpha \cdot d \cdot k} \qquad (equ\ 24)$

"h" is near zero, therefore fiscal policy multiplier is small and changes in Government independent expenditure would not able to affect income considerably.

2.4.2 Monetary Policy Efficiency

By regarding to Figure 12, if LM curve be near to vertical condition (in Sanction condition), Changes in LM curve would affect income at the maximum level but it is necessary to survey IS curve in Target because generally, the slope of IS & LM curves can affect income.

The slope of IS would follow two factors:

1. The amount of Multiplier (K): Increasing "k", would decrease the slope of IS curve thus has more effects on income.

2. Sensibility of investment with regard to changing interest rate (d): Increasing "d" , would decrease the slope of IS curve.

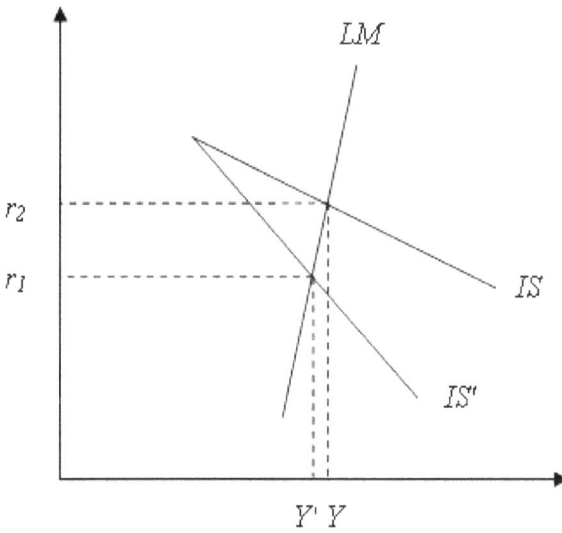

(Fig. 12)

Government income in Sanction condition would decrease significantly, hence Government would increase tax rate. An increase in tax rate, would decrease multiplier and the slope of IS curve, therefore National Income would not be affected such as a period of time before Sanctions.

2.4.3 Unemployment & Inflation

a) The relation between inflation and unemployment: Government operations should be assessed by these two main Economic indexes so that Governments can acquire public trust by controlling these indexes. Generally, unemployment and inflation have reverse relation (Phillips curve):

$$P = AC + yAC \qquad (equ\ 25)$$

Goods price "P" is equal with average cost " AC " plus a percentage of average cost (yAC) as margin profit. On the other hand if wages consider as the cost of production, we would have:

$$AC = \frac{W}{AP_N} \qquad (equ\ 26)$$

$$P = \frac{W}{AP_N} + y\frac{W}{AP_N} = (1+y)\frac{W}{AP_N} \qquad (equ\ 27)$$

In order to achieve inflation rate, we should take Napierian logarithm from two sides then use Total derivative:

$$LnP = Ln(1+ y) + LnW - LnAP_N \qquad \textit{(equ 28)}$$

$$dP/P = dW/W - dAP_N/AP_N \qquad \textit{(equ 29)}$$

$$\dot{P} = \dot{w} - A\dot{P}_N \qquad \textit{(equ 30)}$$

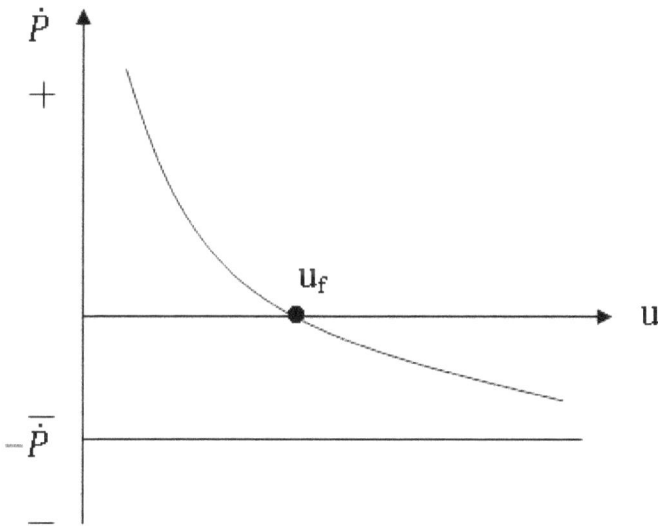

(Fig. 13)

Inflation rate has direct relation with the wages growth rate ($\dot{w}$) and it has inverse relation with the growth of labor yield rate ($A\dot{P}_N$). On the other hand we know that wages growth rate has inverse relation with unemployment rate (u).

Imposing Sanction would decreases labor yield and increases inflation, therefore there is a doubt about inverse relation between inflation rate and unemployment rate in Sanction condition.

Sanctions can aggravate two kinds of inflation:

1. Cost-push inflation

2. Structural inflation

b) *Cost-push inflation:* Increasing price and the shortage of primary materials after Sanctions, would decrease the usage of these materials. If primary materials be considered as a kind of input, in short time a decline in usage of primary materials would decrease the level of production for each amount of labor force employment which can show this event by shifting product function to below. On the other hand it is expected to encounter with a decrease in labor demand because in short time a decline in the usage of primary materials lead to a decrease in marginal product of labor.

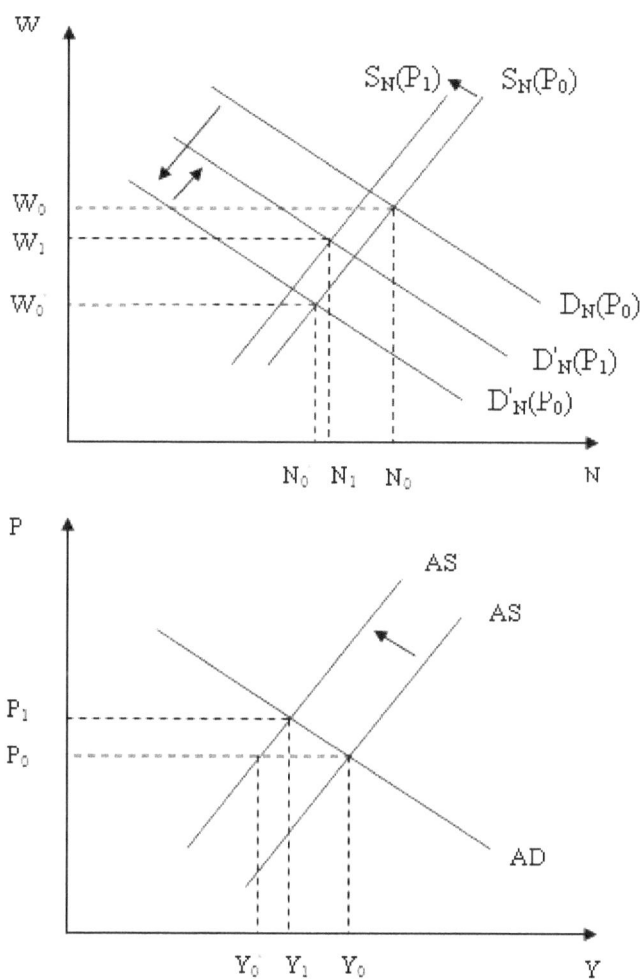

(Fig. 14)

Figure 14 shows that an increase in price of primary materials would shifts product function to below, therefore the demand of labor force would be decreased and shifts $D_N(P_0)$ to $D'_N(P_0)$. A decrease in occupation to the level of N_0' and shifting product function, would decrease the level of production to Y'_0. Therefore at the level of "P_0", the level of total production would be decreased to Y'_0 which may result in excess demand and surging prices. An increase of prices would be continued until the demand and supply of labor force would be equal. Increasing the prices would shifts demand and supply curves so that the level of occupation would be at N_1 and its related production would be at Y_1.

Increasing the price of primary materials would increase the level of general prices thus the level of production and occupation would decrease which result in unemployment. Hence cost-push inflation after Sanctions lead to stagflation.

c) Structural inflation: Factors like Economic structure, political systems, culture and ... can result in this kind of inflation. Structural inflation generally can be seen in developing countries and at the majority of time it cannot be control by fiscal and monetary policies.

There are various reasons that aggravate structural inflation such as Expanded Government, insufficient sub constructions, the weakness of private sectors, continued Government budget deficit, insufficient convenient paths for transportation. for example, with growth of the Government size, many unnecessary organization would be established which need labor force. These employees are not productive whist have the power of purchasing, it means that demand would be increased but supply would encounter with difficulties.

Imposing embargo on trade leads to a decrease at the level of production because the price of primary materials would be increased and supply curve would shifts to left, on the other hand Target would not able to import goods. Imposing a ban on the shipping insurance, is another tool for declining the National production by increasing the costs of transportation. Agencies would sack their workers at this condition thus unemployment rate would increase unexpectedly. Governments with increasing its independent expenditure, would try to increase production and employment but if Governments increase unproductive jobs in its structure, this policy would not be successful and structural inflation would increase considerably.

d) Inflation, unemployment and Supply - Side Economics: Supply-side policies leads to an increase in aggregate supply and demand while fiscal and monetary policies result in changing aggregate demand. One of the main supply-side policies is controlling the level of prices and wages in order to harness inflation which is called income policy. It is necessary to argue that if wages have increased proportionate to labor yield, an increase in aggregate demand would not affect the level of general prices thus country would not experience high inflation. Changes which result in Monopoly failure and competitive condition can be assumed as a supply-side policies because it can shift aggregate supply curve to the right and consequently decreases unemployment so that National production would increase and inflation can be controlled.

The most important supply-side policy is providing incentives for increasing activities and functions through an decrease in tax rate. This policy is not a simple expansionary fiscal policy while it can motivate and increase aggregate supply because it can increase aggregate demand in addition to persuading labors to supply their services.

Figure 15 denotes that initially Government can decrease anarchy by increasing the tax rate because judicial organization and security systems would be extended, therefore suitable atmosphere entice people to work at market but after t* tax has inverse effect on production and with regarding to a decline in production, Government income would decrease dramatically.

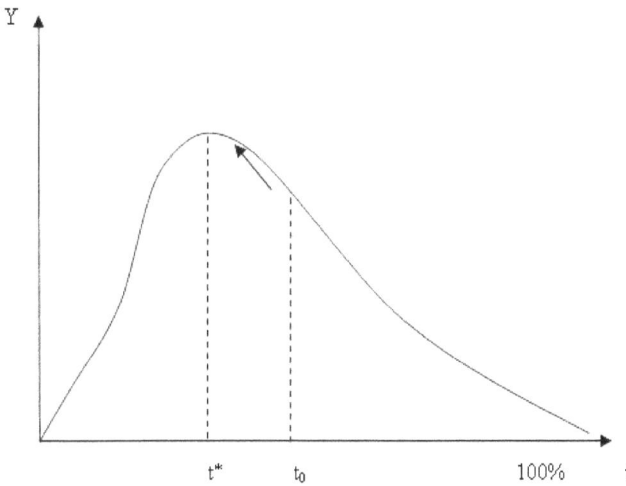

(Fig. 15)

We can survey the effects of above policy by aggregate supply and demand.

A decrease in tax rate would shifts AD to right and on the other hand motivate activities and shifts AS to right too. If curves move the same distances, the level of prices would be stayed without any changes but National Income would increase to the level of Y1, therefore this policy can decrease unemployment and control inflation.

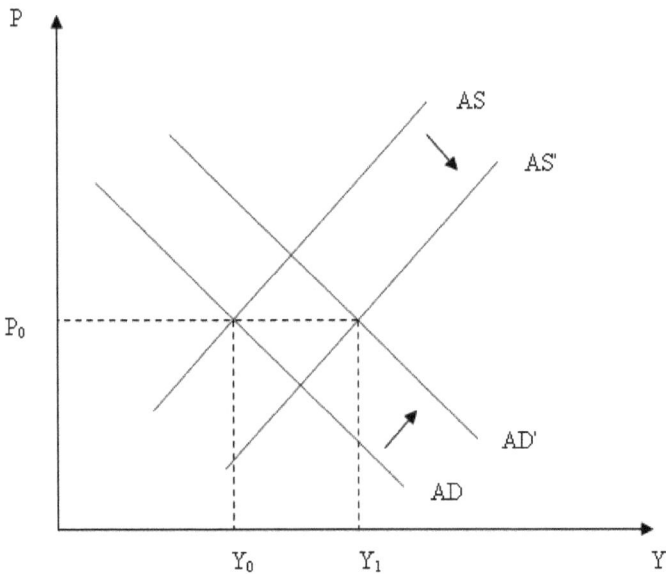

(Fig. 16)

Supply-side Economics would loses its efficiency in the Sanction condition because imposing embargo on import means the shortage of primary materials and Government tax policies would not able to persuade people for increasing their activities at markets. Therefore it is clear that these policies would increase the level of general prices although the slope of AD curve should be taken into consideration. On the other hand after decreasing the tax rate, Government would loses a sheer volume of tax incomes due to a decline in tax rate and production.

2.5 Disordering in Production Factors Market

Production factors encompass environmental sources, labor force, capital and entrepreneurship. we want to survey the role of labor force and production function in Sanction condition.

Aggregate supply and demand determine the level of prices and each changing at the level of prices would affect on labor force supply and demand. The combination of capital and labor force can show various levels of production, therefore production function would determines different level of production if we assume that the volume of capital is constant. The relation between the level of prices and production which is related by labor force market, would shows aggregate supply. The slope and the movement of aggregate supply curve would affect on amount of production and welfare.

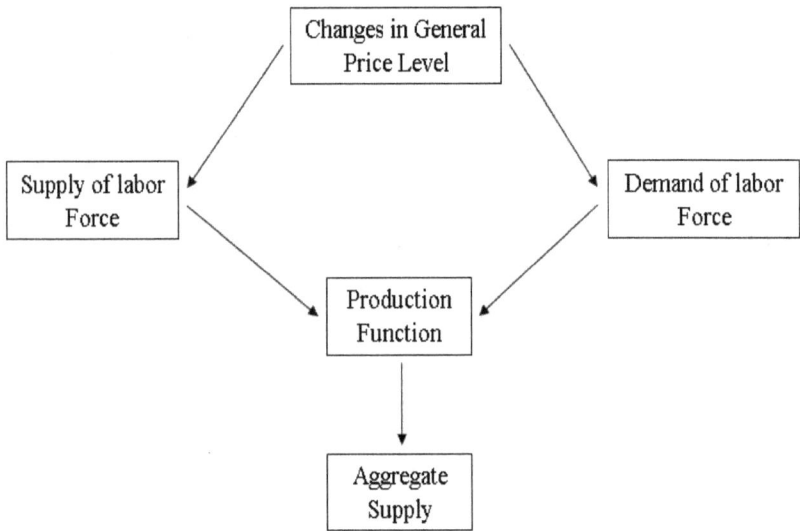

(Fig. 17)

Four factors influence the slope of aggregate supply curve:

1. The slope of labor force supply curve

2. The slope of labor force demand curve

3. The slope of production function

4. Money illusion

Five factors influence the movement of aggregate supply curve:

1. The movement of labor force supply with the constancy of prices.

2. Technology improvement which shifts production function and labor force demand to above.

3. Changing capital stock

4. Changing the amount of primary materials usage

5. Increasing the power of monopoly

Sanction is a dynamic factor so that its effects can be various throughout the Sanction period. Figure 18 shows this fact.

If Economy has normal condition, imposing Sanctions would increase risk and uncertainty in society, hence at the beginning of Sanctions, price expectation is a factor for increasing inflation gradually. Labor force, initially, have money illusion but after awhile money illusion would be decreased.

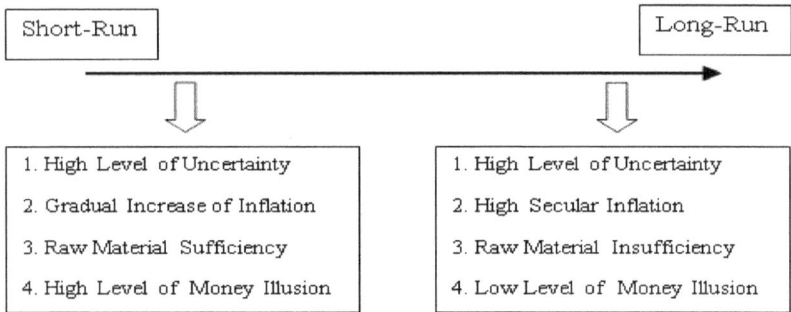

Short-Run	Long-Run
1. High Level of Uncertainty	1. High Level of Uncertainty
2. Gradual Increase of Inflation	2. High Secular Inflation
3. Raw Material Sufficiency	3. Raw Material Insufficiency
4. High Level of Money Illusion	4. Low Level of Money Illusion

(Fig. 18)

On the other hand production function by regarding to the shortage of capital and primary materials, would be changed and it means changing in aggregate supply which may result in an decline in National production. As you see in Figure 19, the level of price is P_0 and the level of production is Y_0 by regarding to $SN(P_0)$ and $DN(P_0)$ which are labor force supply and demand curves respectively also aggregate supply is shown by AS.

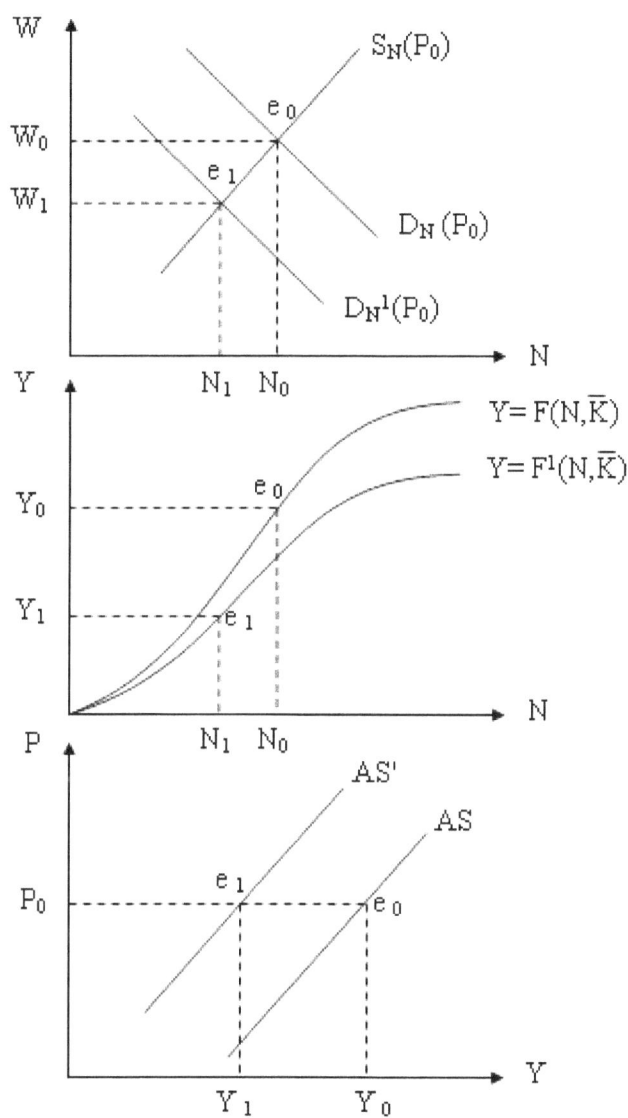

(Fig. 19)

A decrease in marginal product of labor force after Sanctions, would shifts demand curve to left thus occupation would decline to the level of N_1 and production would decline to Y_1, hence aggregate supply would cross the point of e_1 which is shown by AS'.

2.6 Disordering in Households Operation

Households affect Economy by their consumption and saving. Consumption changing can influence demand and National production, also people can affect supply by their saving which constitute necessary sources for investment.

Making decision about consumption depends on individual income as well as peers group's income and consumption. This attitude is known as Demonstration Effect. Therefore individuals who have lower consumption than average consumption, would try to arrive this level of consumption while more proportion of income would pay if they have lower income in comparison to others.

Individuals after falling into the habit of specific consumption, would not able to quit this level of consumption. This model is known as Ratchet Effect. Consumption function can be shown as:

$$C = aD + cY + bDY \qquad (equ\ 31)$$

$$a > 0\ ,\ 0 < c < 1\ ,\ b < 0\ ,\ |b| < c \qquad (equ\ 32)$$

$$D\begin{cases} = 1 & if \quad Y > Y_0 \\ = 0 & if \quad Y < Y_0 \end{cases} \qquad (equ\ 33)$$

$$if\ D = 1 \qquad\qquad C = a + (b + c)\,Y \qquad (equ\ 34)$$

$$if\ D = 0 \qquad\qquad\qquad C = cY \qquad (equ\ 35)$$

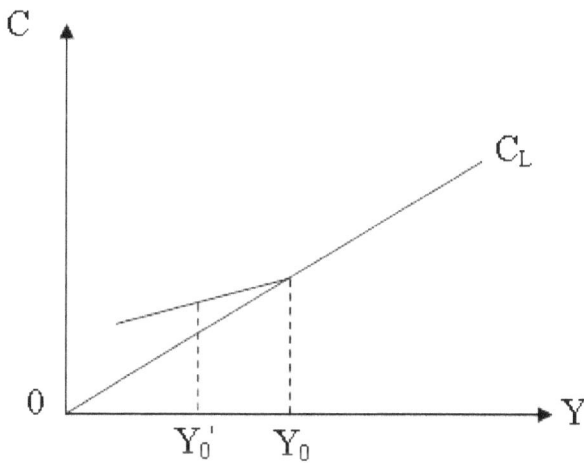

(Fig. 20)

After decreasing income, consumption would not moves on the previous curve and it would transfer on a curve with lower slope. Sanction is a factor which would decline individuals income, therefore it is expected to see a decrease in consumption but with lower slope.

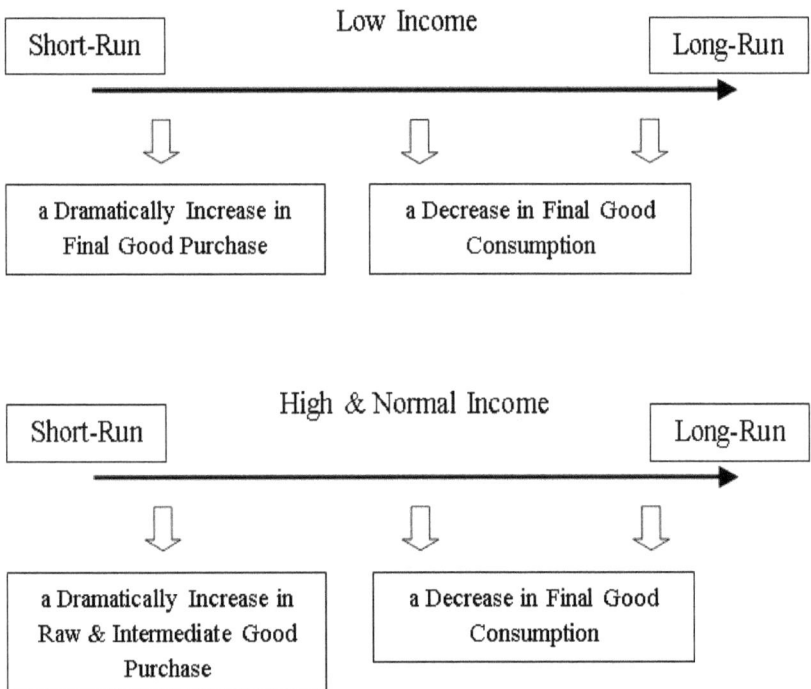

(Fig. 21)

Sanctions would increase uncertainty and inflation expectation in society. People with low income because of inflation expectation would increase their goods demand by their saving at the beginning of Sanction, therefore Target would experience high inflation but throughout the sanction period people would lose their purchasing power thus this inflation would not affects goods supply and the level of production.

People with normal income would spend amount of their wealth on goods at the beginning of Sanction but by regarding to their forecasting about future, individuals would buy primary and final goods for hoarding and acquiring profit.

Individuals with low income would lose their saving power in Sanction condition because income is equal with consumption and saving, therefore after decreasing income, consumption would not be decreased with previous slope thus saving would be declined gradually. On the other hand individuals with normal and high income, would spend a sheer volume of money for purchasing gold and foreign currency in order to prevent the negative effects of inflation, therefore total amount of saving would be decreased and suitable investment would not be accessible. (Stagflation condition)

2.7 Disordering in Foreign Sector Operation

Imposing embargo on trade would decrease Economic relations with Target but for preventing Sanction failure, Senders should control all related sectors.

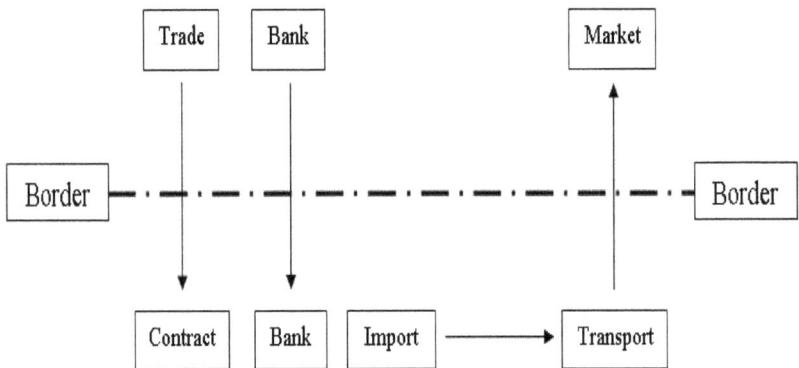

(Fig. 22)

Figure 22 shows the process of import. Trader for contract should travel to foreign countries and after signing the contract they should pay money through banks and finally goods should be transported to Target.

Sanction has plan for each part, initially Sender(s) would imposing ban on travelling thus traders should trust foreign firms from afar. On the other hand traders would not able to choose the best market and sellers want to have a monopoly, therefore the level of prices would increase dramatically. Traders would encounter with many difficulties for charging sellers bank account, hence traders would transfer money in cash or indirectly (Through bilateral country) which can increase the costs. Goods transportation to Target is another barrier which increases the costs, imposing embargo on shipping insurance would surge the cost of transportation, also cargos cannot transport directly and initially it should enters bilateral country. Therefore final price of goods would rises considerably.

The Game Of Sanction

Introduction

Two sides of each Sanction would use suitable strategies like chess player, therefore dynamic Sanction is a reason which decreases the efficiency of monetary and fiscal policy.

Sender(s) should make provision for Sanctions. It is clear that comprehensive Sanction needs international support, therefore powerful foreign policy is the main part of each sweeping measures.

1. Sender(s) Plays Role Like White Chessman

Sender(s) shows the first action such as constituting international rally against Target. Sender(s) at the first step would imposing a ban on the trade of weapons because this power act as a deterrent against Sanctions. Obviously, Target after these signs would collects its assets from foreign countries, therefore it is of great necessity to freezing assets after the first step.

Changing regime or attitudes can be happened through two factors:

1. Direct pressure on Government

2. Indirect pressure on Government through people

Imposing a ban on high-ranks travelling as well as freezing assets can change their attitudes but generally increasing pressure on people can work as complement solution.

Uncertainty is the most important factor which can destroy Economic structure but people would conform to new condition after a period of time, therefore Sender(s) should manage time and utilize various strategies for preventing any conformity.

The majority of time, Sanctions have different stages so that after each stage Sender(s) would survey reactions of Target in order to error correcting. Each kind of Sanction has specific results thus the optimum combination of diverse Sanctions can be different against various countries. Sometimes Sender(s) would provide various incentives for Target in order to change the atmosphere and persuade Target to change a behavior.

Figure 23 shows that each kind of Sanction impose pressure on specific sectors although each sanction can broaden to other sectors with a lag of time.

Imposing a ban on the trade of weapons, academic relations and travelling are Sanction tools for warning but these tools do not have enough power which coerce Target into changing attitudes.

Factors of Sanction	The First Effect	The Second Effect
Weapon	Gov.	---
Travelling	Gov. - Firms	People
Technology	Gov. - Firms	People
Finance	Gov. - Firms	People
Academic Relations	Gov. - People	---
Bank	Gov. - Firms - People	---
Export	Gov. - Firms - People	---
Import of Raw Materials	Gov. - Firms	People
Import of Final Goods	Gov. - Firms - People	---
Gold & Jewel	Gov.	Firms - People
Transportation	Gov. - Firms	People
Insurance	Gov. - Firms	People

Gov. = Government

(Fig. 23)

Imposing a ban on transport insurance would increases the costs of import and export thus it would increases inflation.

Imposing embargo on banks, gold and jewels would increase difficulties for continuing the process of purchasing from foreign countries so that the Economy of Target would not bear this condition.

Freezing assets and finance as well as imposing a ban on technologies can prevent new modern industrial projects with high efficiency so that increasing the cost of production and inefficient industry can coerce Government into accepting requests of Sender(s).

Imposing embargo on import and export of goods can be the last stage of each Sanction which may result in tragic events, therefore international humanistic NGO's would prevent this condition.

Encouragement and punishment are two sides of each Sanction which would acquire the best results if Sender(s) utilize suitable combination of these tools. Providing incentives can reduce unexpected reactions from Target, on the other hand it can entice people to force Government in order to accept Sender(s) requests.

2. Target Plays Role Like Black Chessman

Punishment Sanctions such as military Sanctions can be considered as warning, hence Target would make policies for reducing the consequences of comprehensive Sanctions. Comparative advantages show the structure of production in each country but Sanction would imposing a ban on import and export, therefore it is necessary for Target to import new technologies before comprehensive Sanctions although the process of making decision about new considerable budget for purchasing new technologies would take long time. It is clear that Sanction is a kind of Game which depends on Time.

Expectation inflation in Sanction condition is the main reason which increase inflation, therefore Government can decrease this effect by making some prices stable because it can send positive signals to consumers. On the other hand Target cannot import essential goods thus Government should supply these goods with low costs. But how?

Each country has considerable Economic potential which is useless in peaceful condition. The Army in each country has cheap and powerful facilities as well as free labor force which are broadened throughout country. In Sanction condition by regarding to an absence of production in some sectors, Government should uses Army to product cheap goods on the other hand transportation by Armies' facilities can reduce the cost of final goods. There is no doubt that Army should spends their time for producing raw and mediate goods because private sectors can product final goods more efficiently.

Imposing embargo on banks would change ties between Target and sellers. Gold and valuable stones can be used as money with Target, therefore banks of Gold and foreign currency can be a main solution for Target which absorb gold and foreign currency from people.

Refferences

W.H. Branson; Macroeconomic Theory and Policy, Third Edition; 1989.

T. Rahmani; Macroeconomics, Sixth Edition; 2004.

M. Roozbahan; Macroeconomic Theory, 25th Edition; 2004.

T. Sandler & K. Hartley; Handbook of Defense Economics, Volume 2, 2007.

P.Wonnacott & R. Wonnacott; What's the point of Reciprocal Trade Negotiations? Exports, Imports and Gains From Trade; Blackwell, 2005.

R. Caruso; The Impact of International Economic Sanctions on Trade An empirical Analysis, European Peace Science Conference, 2003.

E. Carter; International Economic Sanctions: Improving the
Haphazard U.S. Legal Regime; California Law Review, 1987.

J. Galtung; On the Effects of International Economic Sanctions: With Examples from the Case of Rhodesia; World politics, Volume 19, Issue 3 (Apr.,1967)

www.ingramcontent.com/pod-product-compliance
Lightning Source LLC
Chambersburg PA
CBHW071602200326
41519CB00021BB/6838